DEHUMANIZING WOMEN

NEW FEMINIST PERSPECTIVES
Edited by Mary Vetterling-Braggin

BEYOND DOMINATION
New Perspectives on Women and Philosophy
Carol C. Gould, editor

MOTHERING
Essays in Feminist Theory
Joyce Trebilcot, editor

WOMEN AND SPIRITUALITY
Carol Ochs

WOMEN, SEX, AND THE LAW
Rosemarie Tong

DEHUMANIZING WOMEN

Treating Persons as
Sex Objects

Linda LeMoncheck

Rowman & Allanheld
PUBLISHERS

ROWMAN & ALLANHELD

Published in the United States of America in 1985
by Rowman & Allanheld, Publishers
(A division of Littlefield, Adams & Company)
81 Adams Drive, Totowa, New Jersey 07512

Copyright © 1985 by Rowman & Allanheld, Publishers

Library of Congress Cataloging in Publication Data

LeMoncheck, Linda
  Dehumanizing women.

  Bibliography: p.
  Includes index.
  1. Sex role—Moral and ethical aspects.
2. Interpersonal relations—Moral and ethical
aspects. 3. Sexism. I. Title.
HQ1075.L45 1984   305.3   84-17905
ISBN 0-8476-7331-6
ISBN 0-8476-7386-3 (pbk.)

84 85 86 / 10 9 8 7 6 5 4 3 2 1

Printed in the United States of America

*This book is dedicated to all the women
in search of both a sympathetic ear and an analytic eye
concerning the problem of sex objectification.*

Contents

Preface

This book was written in an attempt to fill a conspicuous gap in both the contemporary feminist and philosophical literature by creating a systematic and critical account of treating women (and men) as sex objects. Its method is that of analytic moral philosophy tempered by feminist insight. It speaks to the requirements of analytic moral philosophy by inquiring about what it means to treat someone, woman or man, as a sex object, what (if anything) is wrong with such treatment, and what we should do about righting any wrong that does occur. As such, it is intended to be both useful and accessible to the introductory student of philosophy as a text in contemporary normative ethics, yet it is also directed to the more advanced philosopher interested in the ways in which her or his craft may be used to explore some important areas of feminist concern, specifically those of sexism and sex stereotypes as well as the general area of sex objectification. In this sense, the book is also intended to show feminists the light that philosophical inquiry can shed on their own social and political positions.

However, we will not ignore the emotional component of sex objectification. This book uses the analytic method to clear the conceptual and moral confusion often caused by the short fuse of emotion, but the analysis would remain in the realm of theory only, distant and ultimately useless as a learning tool, if it did not speak to the real frustrations, anxieties, anger, and hostility that women and men feel on both sides of the issue. Thus, the discussion offers several paradigm examples of women treated as sex objects in an attempt to use their reactions as a basis for a conceptual and moral analysis of the treatment they experience. This analysis is meant to help those women who do feel victimized by sex objectification to understand their feelings and to articulate clearly their complaints; it is meant to help those men who do not hear or understand those complaints to listen with a more comprehending ear; and it is meant to help both women and men see the extent to which the prevailing social, economic, and political oppression of women, of which women's sex objectification is a part, fosters and reinforces relations between the sexes that are anathema to both.

A note about word usage: because women constitute the paradigmatic "sex objects" in contemporary society, and because it is to their complaints that any comprehensive moral analysis of sex objectification must speak, the pronoun "she" is used throughout the discussion when the sex of the sex object remains otherwise unspecified. There is no logical contradiction, however, in the expression "male sex object," and as we shall see, relations of status and power between persons can be so structured as to turn a male sex partner into a male sex object. Thus, the analysis in Chapter I of the dehumanization involved in sex objectification is couched in terms of treating "persons," not only women, as sex objects. This is not in any way to imply that the problems that women have with being treated as sex objects, given the prevailing sexual ideology and patriarchal social climate, are exactly similar to any problems that men might have, and Chapter II examines some of the important asymmetries that exist between the two forms of treatment, asymmetries that reflect our current sexual double standard of the aggressive subject male versus the passive object female, as well as the current politically subordinate position of women in or out of sex. The point of examining the problems with treating any one person as a sex object, then, is not to blur this asymmetry but to capture the wrong that women presently suffer, a wrong that anyone, woman or man, should not be caused to suffer, and that men are not presently made to suffer with the same frequency, indignity, or larger social implications.

Finally, as a white, middle-class, educated, heterosexual woman and feminist, it would be naive to profess any kind of so-called objectivity to the analysis below; indeed, I do not think such a perspective exists, since as inquiring subject one must assume a perspective from which to launch the inquiry. Some feminists have even argued that to profess objectivity is to adopt the sexist stance of inquiring active Self (male) passing judgment on his object of study, the purported alien and inactive Other (female), a stance that is unacceptable because it "objectifies" the Other. Catharine MacKinnon, in "Feminism, Marxism, Method, and the State: An Agenda for Theory," (*Signs: Journal of Women in Culture and Society* 7, No. 3 Spring, 1982, pp. 536ff.) writes, "Having been objectified as sexual beings while being stigmatized as ruled by subjective passions, women reject the distinction between knowing subject and known object — the division between subjective and objective postures — as the means to comprehend social life." As a woman and feminist I am sympathetic to the complaints of the sex object and see them as symptomatic, if not definitive, of women's broader social, economic and political oppression. As a white, middle-class, educated heterosexual I will very probably fail to identify some of the features of sex objectification that are unique to members of other races, classes, or sexual orientation. Indeed, for those persons, sex objectification of the kind described below may not even be a pressing feminist issue. (Feminism itself has been accused of race and class bias. For some of the ways in which race and class affect one's perceptions of feminism, *see* Bonnie Thornton's "Race, Class, and Gender: Prospects for an All-Inclusive Sisterhood," in *Feminist Studies* 9, No. 1 Spring, 1983.) I consider it at least a step in the right direction to be aware of the limitations on my thinking that such a position must impose, and my hope is that such limitations will be used to stimulate further discussion on the subject and ultimately to broaden the social perspectives of us all.

Acknowledgments

There are several people who should be given special recognition for their continued interest in and support for my research into treating both women and men as sex objects. First, I wish to express my gratitude to Thomas E. Hill, Jr. for first introducing me to the philosophical complexities of sex objectification as well as for reading the several drafts that comprised my UCLA philosophy dissertation on the subject. Richard Wasserstrom was kind enough to read those same drafts while chairing the philosophy department at the University of California, Santa Cruz, setting time aside for several long-distance telephone conferences and traveling south to sit on my orals committee. For reading my preliminary prospectus on sex objectification and helping me sharpen the focus of my arguments, I also wish to thank Barbara Gutek, Ann Peplau, and Herbert Morris. To Al Spangler I wish to extend a special appreciation for giving me the confidence and courage to seek publication of the dissertation. To those who also read the dissertation after completion and helped me clarify and edit further, Ann Garry, Ed Quest, and Ben Freedman, I offer sincere thanks. To Alison Jaggar I owe my introduction to feminist theory and the tenets of socialist feminism in particular. And to Mary Vetterling-Braggin I offer my thanks for her incisive editorship and for exposing much of the subtle but identifiable sexism left in my own writing.

In addition, I extend my warmest thanks for a careful and critical review of my work to all those who were interested enough to attend and/or contribute to a discussion of sex objectification and sex stereotyping at a presentation of papers on those topics for the Pacific APA meetings in Sacramento in April, 1982, the Occidental College Feminist Fortnight, January, 1983, and the California State University, Long Beach Philosophy Colloquium Series in the fall of 1981 and spring of 1983. To my family and friends goes my appreciation for their moral support throughout the writing of this book amidst their own busy lives. Jed Shafer has been essential for my self-esteem and self-confidence throughout this project, a self-proclaimed "man behind the woman" who has shown me that emotional dependence on, and independence of, other people are both legitimate sides of the same feminist coin. To all the authors listed in the bibliography I express my gratitude for their insights and inspirations, without which this book could not have been written (but to whom none of the errors should be attributed). And finally, to all those women and men alike who shared with me their fears and frustrations, their anger and angst over sex and sexism: my hope in writing this book was not so much to allay those feelings but to give them clarity, substance, and credibility.

Introduction

Women often complain that they dislike being treated as sex objects. When asked what provides the grounds for such complaints, they generally reply in the form of the N.O.W. affirmation that such regard is simply "degrading" to women[1] and as such is objectionable on those grounds alone. But does this reply capture all that might be objectionable about this phenomenon? Are there any examples of treating someone as a sex object — what has been referred to as "sex objectification"[2] — that are not objectionable at all? Are some cases more objectionable than others? What, if anything, should we do to eliminate the problem cases? Even more fundamental, what is this phenomenon of sex objectification in the first place?

The aim of the following discussion is to examine critically the nature of, and objections to, treating persons as sex objects. In Chapter I, a preliminary characterization of sex objectification is developed, a characterization based on three typical examples of treating a woman as a sex object. In Chapter II, the characterization introduced in Chapter I is tested against a wider variety of cases than those described previously. Specifically, Chapter I describes three cases of women who complain about being treated as sex objects by men. Chapter II examines such cases as those of men who are treated as sex objects by both women and other men, persons who treat themselves as sex objects, and people who permit, consent to, or recommend their own sex objectification by others. These cases further illuminate the nature of sex objectification characterized in Chapter I. Also included in Chapter II is an exploration of the special significance that the prevailing

sexual attitudes of contemporary society have for any moral evaluation we might give to sex objectification followed by an examination
of the claim that treating women as sex objects is an instance of sexist
treatment. This latter discussion offers an analysis of what it means to
stereotype a person according to her or his sex; in particular, it details
the relationship between a sex stereotype and the different role expectations persons have for both sexes when they find one sex or the other
sexually attractive or sexually stimulating. Chapter III compares the
resulting characterization of sex objectification with those that other
philosophers have offered. Finally, Chapter IV asks the question of
whether or not the woman who consents to her sex objectification by
others in contemporary society is morally justified in doing so. The
conclusion offers one ideal in human sexual relations consistent with
the earlier observations on sex objectification as well as suggestions
about some of the areas we must attack if we are to instigate the sorts of
social changes that would approach this ideal. I also speculate as to
the probabilities of success for such changes and whether some success
is better than none at all.

The thesis of the book is that treating persons as sex objects involves
treating persons as less than the moral equals of other persons. Someone who is treated as a sex object, in other words, is someone whose
sexual attraction or sexuality is used by the sex objectifier as the vehicle for treating that person as deserving less of the rights or none of the
rights to well-being and freedom that other persons enjoy. Such a
characterization not only appears to be consistent with the wide variety of types of sex objectification that exist, it can also be used to explain both why someone would complain about her or his sex objectification to begin with as well as what the specific content of those
complaints might be. In addition, such a characterization can be used
to explain why someone might not even complain at all about the
treatment she or he receives. To account for such cases, the rights to
well-being and freedom discussed in Chapter I are defined as such
that they may be appropriately overridden or waived under special
circumstances. Furthermore, the characterization allows that there
may be those non-complainers who do not value their rights to well-
being and freedom or those who would not regard their treatment as
sex objectification on my model, since they do not believe any rights
of theirs are being violated at all. In Chapter IV however it is argued
that there is a strong probability that the woman in contemporary so-

ciety who is valued by others primarily for her ability to attract or stimulate men sexually is not being treated as the moral equal of other persons in her society.

A notable feature of this analyis of sex objectification is that the moral evaluations made of the phenomenon are not arrived at first by adopting some prevailing moral theory, such as a theory of utility or a theory of justice as fairness, secondly by justifying its use, and then thirdly by applying it to the cases under consideration. In fact, the concluding paragraphs of the book suggest that a specifically sexual morality demands the kind of investigation which is not properly covered by independent moral considerations alone, but also by considerations of the prevailing social context and sexual ideology under which the sex objectification occurs. Therefore, the analysis below proceeds first by presenting the considered judgments of those who are treated as sex objects and secondly by asking what moral principles seem to underlie these judgments. Then after investigating the social context in which such principles are endorsed, we are in a position to assess whether or not such principles are viable within that context. No metaethical arguments are offered for the claim that moral principles should be analyzed along the context-specific lines mentioned above or that we can ever conclusively justify the moral principles we do adopt. I take this to be the task of a separate work. Nevertheless, at the very least the moral claims of this book can be understood in the form of the hypothetical, viz. *if* we accept such principles as those endorsed in this book, *then* the phenomenon of treating persons as sex objects should be evaluated along the lines described.

I have not formally established a statistical data base which empirically verifies the considered judgments I discuss. This is the job of the sociologist and social psychologist, not the philosopher. What I have done is to report those judgments which it is plausible to think that persons do in fact make, and which the author's limited observations suggest persons do make. I believe these judgments are of wide enough range and depth for me to be able to claim a satisfactory minimum of factual accuracy, at least for the purposes of this book. Any descriptive task for the philosopher in this area is to display clearly and coherently the formal and normative variety to be found in treating persons as sex objects and to characterize sex objectification based on that variety. Furthermore, this task is a necessary preliminary to evaluating the normative accuracy of the considered judgments persons make of what has been characterized as sex object-ification.

In short, the aims of the book are as follows: (1) to clarify what the phenomenon of sex objectification is by exhibiting the variety of cases that there are; (2) to explain why it is that some persons complain about their sex objectificaiion while others do not by investigating both the conceptual and normative claims which underlie such reactions; (3) to indicate the direction which our moral judgments should take for any one case we confront, provided that we do accept the resulting characterization of sex objectification and the moral principles which underlie it offered here; and (4) to suggest what, if anything, should be done to right any wrong or prevent any offense caused by treating persons as sex objects.

NOTES

1 *L.A. Times* November 4, 1979.

2 Treating a woman as a sex object has been referred to as "sex objectification" by Sandra Lee Bartky in her article, "On Psychological Oppression" in *Philosophy and Women,* ed. Sharon Bishop and Marjorie Weinzweig (Belmont, California: Wadsworth Publishing Company, 1979), pp. 33–41.

chapter 1

The Nature of the Complaint

1. A STRATEGY FOR CHARACTERIZING SEX OBJECTIFICATION

One of the challenges of a thorough analysis of sex objectification is the wide variety of opinion of what that actually is, variety both in the nature or form which the sex objectification takes and in the normative evaluations that persons make of it. For example, both the practice of raping a woman and the mental act of merely fantasizing about her sexual merits have each been called treating her as a sex object. And both the act of whistling at a woman standing on a street corner and whistling at a woman performing a striptease have been considered by different people to be inappropriate, permissible, or recommended. What appears clear from the outset is that treating a woman as a sex object can mean either conceiving of her as a sex object or acting toward her as a sex object—or both—and it is clear that any one case of sex objectification may be at once objectionable to some and enjoyable to others. Thus, any satisfactory characterization of sex objectification we offer should be broad enough in scope to account for such variety.

We will construct such a characterization first by examining three "typical" ("complaint") cases, then generalizing over those cases on the basis of the variety of complaints contained within them. We want to develop a characterization that can explain why some persons might complain about being treated as sex objects while others might not, as well as why someone might make the particular complaints she does and not other complaints instead. So, for example, we not only want a characterization that would account for the fact that some people find sex objectification demeaning and some do not, but one that shows why sex objectification might be construed as demeaning at all, as distinct from being viewed as uncharitable or spiteful or simply inconvenient.

A comprehensive account of sex objectification should also speak to those instances in which persons do not complain about being treated as sex objects, including those in which persons attest that they thoroughly enjoy the treatment.[1] How can a characterizaton of sex objectification with what appears to be negative normative weight attached be able to account for those cases in which persons do not object? We need not characterize sex objectification as always wrong or absolutely inappropriate; we need only say that it is *prima facie* inappropriate, viz. inappropriate unless it can be shown that special competing considerations justify the treatment.[2] In this way, cases of what appear to be sex objectification may be considered unobjectionable by persons and still be accurately characterized as cases of sex objectification. What the *prima facie* claim implies is that the burden is on those who do not think it inappropriate to show why.[3] This way of characterizing sex objectification is similar to defining lying as "the *prima facie* inappropriate telling of falsehoods" or defining murder as "the *prima facie* inappropriate killing of the innocent" instead of defining such terms neutrally, as "telling falsehoods" and "killing the innocent." While it is typically inappropriate to lie or murder, there are cases of what we (accurately) call "lying" and "murder" in which the liar and murderer are morally justified in acting as they do. In light of such considerations, the qualified normative definitions of lying and murder tend to better approximate the considered moral judgments of persons than their normatively neutral counterparts. Likewise, a characterization of sex objectification with *prima facie* negative normative weight attached most accurately mirrors the spectrum of considered judgments that persons make of sex objectification. It allows us consistently to say that persons may have good reasons for consenting to their own sex objectification, even when we assume the typical case to be one to which no one would consent. And if some persons do not think their treatment is even *prima facie* objectionable, we can ask whether or not their treatment should be called 'sex objectification' at all.

However, as we suggested in the introduction, it is one sort of enterprise to formulate and explain the sorts of considered normative judgments that persons do in fact make of sex objectification and quite another to ask whether those judgments are ones that persons ought in fact to make. The former task is partly one of gathering factual data (What do people say?), partly one of conceptual clarification (What do people mean by what they say?), and partly one of moral clarification (What moral principles, if any, underlie what people say?). The latter task is one of normative evaluation, of deciding which considered judgments and principles we ought to accept. Thus, the addition of the expression *prima facie* to describe the apparent inappropriateness of sex objectification is only to make the characterization of sex objectification match what persons do in fact think about their own and others' sex objectification. However, we may later discover that many of those same reasons persons believe justify sex objectification do not in fact justify it, or justify it only inconclusively. The task of examining whether or not persons can justify their own and others' sex objectification is taken up in Chapters II and IV.

2. THREE EXAMPLES OF SEX OBJECTIFICATION

Our first case is that of "the free spirit": Imagine a woman in her late teens walking home from school on a bright clear day. Since it is quite warm outside, she is bare-legged, and dressed in a sleeveless cotton sundress and sandals. She walks by a construction site near her house at which three men are working. The minute they see her, one lets out a loud wolf-whistle, one taunts her with "Hey fox, give us a smile!" and the third simply stares in silence, thinking, "Now that's a nice piece of ass!" Grinning broadly, they are full of the self-importance that accompanies seeing themselves as sexually confident initiators of the encounter and as dominators of the action. However the free spirit reacts, she will react to their intrusion and their attention. But the workers do not really expect the free spirit to smile for them on demand, much less stop to investigate their intentions further, although such an investigation would be fully welcomed; nor do they really care whether she takes their attentions as a compliment, although they wonder why so many women do not. In fact, their experience has led them to believe that women only pretend they do not want sex when they really do most of the time. If the women they meet really do not want it, the men contend, then they are just frigid or lesbians. Why, they wonder, would a woman wear a short dress unless she really wanted to show off a good pair of legs? Being coy, they assume, is just part of the feminine role women adopt in any personal encounter they have with men, so why not play the corresponding masculine aggressive role to get the ball rolling? To them, it seems to be the natural order of things.

The free spirit's reaction to the cat calls and comments from the workers is a combination of embarrassment, anger, and fear. She does not really know whether a smile is all they want (she knows that rapes have been initiated, indeed justified, on less); thus, she is afraid to tell them that she thinks what they do is rude and upsetting. She immediately looks down at her dress to be sure it has not fluttered too high above her knees in the wind. She blushes with a self-conscious sense of her own sexuality that she had not had until this moment: "I feel as if they could see right through my dress," she thought. Furthermore, she is angry with herself for not noticing the men soon enough to avoid walking past them; but she is even angrier that she should have to maintain that kind of awareness against men at all. To do so would certainly mean that the freedom and spontaneity which she enjoys in her life would all but disappear. With a sigh, she determines to re-route her walk home from school, even though this particular walk is the shortest and pleasantest, but, she feels helpless to alter her current situation. All she can think to do is to hurry away from the site, flustered and humiliated, while the men return to their work, laughing among themselves. But what she really wanted to do was to walk right up to the construction workers and reply, "Women are a lot more than sex objects, you know!"

Compare this case with the one of "the unhappy wife": A husband and wife, both lawyers, are readying themselves for bed after attending a cocktail party at the home of one of their friends. She is tired, but willing to chat about the events of the evening; he is drunk and wants nothing from her but sex. Not noticing her fatigue, the husband pulls his wife playfully but firmly onto their bed, and in a voice both whining and demanding, says, "C'mon, baby doll, *I* wanna screw." He recalls that she has not been all that willing to have sex with him in the last few months, but she's his *wife,* for Christ's sake, he thinks, and she ought to be willing, yes, even happy to oblige her husband's sexual needs. From the wife's perspective, we can imagine that she is far from in an amorous mood, given her own fatigue and her husband's clumsy gropings and bourbon breath. But she is simply too exhausted to fend off his presumptuous and unwelcome overtures. She never used to be "too tired" for sex when it was sex that she too could enjoy. But she knows that, drunk or sober, there is only one sort of sex her husband seems willing to provide. She recalls John Barth's expression for it: "the two-minute emissionary missionary superior ejaculation service,"[4] and it serves his needs alone, not hers as well. Sex, of all things, she thinks, as her husband lies asleep after the predictable two minutes, should be a shared experience, an intimate exchange of stimulation and satisfaction, not a truncated, one-sided activity. "I might as well put him to bed with a sexually stimulating machine, for all he might care, so long as he is satisfied sexually. Yet he is so attentive at parties. And just this evening, I overheard him bragging about the great defense I presented in court today. Why is it that I'm considered a person when I'm a party companion or a lawyer, but when it comes to sex, I'm nothing more than a feelingless object?"

And finally, note the case of "the assistant manager": The male president of a business firm notices both the sexual attractiveness and the intelligence of a certain female assistant manager working in his office. "Now that's the kind of woman that really turns me on," he muses, "one with a body and brains!" He is doubtful that a married, middle-aged executive is the sort of man to whom she might be sexually attracted, much less the sort with whom she would willingly have an affair. However, he is convinced that the lure of a good promotion can get him what he wants. In light of these facts, the president calls the assistant manager into his office one morning and suggests that he would be willing to promote her to manager of her division if she were to consent to have sex with him at an apartment he is renting near the office. "That's about the only way I know that women get ahead in business," he assures her. And moving closer, he adds, "Besides, sugar, why not mix a little business with pleasure?" The assistant manager, who has worked diligently at her job to qualify for promotion, turns away from him in disgust. She remembers all the times he would "happen by" her office while she was busy; one of the secretaries even told her that she thought she caught the boss giving the assistant manager a long stare up and down her body — the "once-over" — but the assistant manager shrugged it off. He was there to talk business, and she was a woman with a good figure (attractive, she thought), so what's the harm? But now she realized what was inside his head all the time they "talked business." Not business, at all, but sex, sex in exchange for a promotion. "I don't know the guy and I don't want to," she thinks. "What right does he think he has, that he can use me to play with himself? He knows I'm bright, even an economic asset to the company. But that doesn't matter in the end. All I'm good for is sex, sex, sex. I suppose I'm expected to act like some appreciative pet and accept the juicy morsel offered to me. It's as if all this time we've been talking, he's been plotting how to get me in bed — how humiliating!" But she is torn: she deserves her promotion and does not want to resign. (It would only seem to prove his point that women couldn't get ahead without sex.) On the other hand, she cannot tolerate working around men who think of women as servants to their sexual whims. All she can manage to do is walk out the door, sobbing, "I'm sick and tired of men who think women are nothing but sex objects!"

The first thing to notice about the three cases above is that, even though they are all cases of women complaining about being treated as sex objects by men, the circumstances of their sex objectification are very different. For example, in the case of the free spirit, her objectifiers are strangers to her, acting in concert; in the cases of the unhappy wife and assistant manager, they know their objectifiers by name, and their objectifiers act alone. Indeed, the unhappy wife's objectifier is her own husband. Furthermore, the case of the unhappy wife suggests that sex objectification can occur in perfectly appropriate settings for sexual relations; the bedroom is as conducive to such treatment (if not more so) as the boardroom or construction site. Nor does the objectification necessarily involve the public recognition or discussion of a woman's more private body parts; the treatment of the unhappy wife is in the privacy of her own home, even though hers is the only case in which her body is physically exposed. Moreover, unlike the case of the free spirit, the cases of the unhappy wife and assistant manager suggest that no perceived threat of physical harm, much less actual assault, need play any role in the encounter. We can suppose that the wife knows her husband to be of a basically non-violent sort; and the assistant manager may not get promoted for refusing the president, but she does not expect to be assaulted for it.

This is not to suggest that the abruptness of a stranger, the inappropriateness of the context, or the threat of harm are not factors to be considered when assessing what is objectionable about any one case of sex objectification. It is simply to point out that such specific facts cannot appear in any characterization of sex objectification which would attempt to generalize over a variety of cases. In fact, our characterization of sex objectification must also account for the fact that there may be something about sex objectifying thoughts or attitudes as well as their practices that are a source for complaint. For while the husband and company president ultimately feel compelled to confront their sex objects with their demands, the silent, staring construction worker is happy to stand back and grin while his partners carry on. We could even imagine the free spirit walking by the one construction worker completely oblivious to his thoughts about her. Yet, if she were told about the nature of his thoughts after the fact, the free spirit's reaction would very probably take the form that she does not appreciate being thought about that way.

Then what sort of treatment is it that is common to each of the examples above that the women in those examples are complaining about? First, let us note what those who worry about sex objectification do *not* mean by that expression. Following Elizabeth Eames, we must make a distinction between woman as "sex thing" and woman as "object of sexual desire."[5] The term "object" is often used in the sense of "objective" or "something intended or aimed at" such as "objects of attention," "objects of affection," or "objects of effort and organization." When "sex object" is translated "sexual objective" or "aim of sexual desire" or even "someone to have sex with," it does not carry with it the necessary disapprobation that many women claim it has. It is quite plausible to suppose, for example, that the free spirit, the unhappy wife, and the assistant manager all enjoy sexual intercourse, but nevertheless dislike being treated as sex objects. As we shall discover in section 5 of this chapter, it is only when women are regarded as inanimate objects, bodies, or animals, where their status as the moral equals of persons has been demeaned or degraded, that the expression "sex objectification" is correctly used. This confusion seems to be the source of the mistaken belief on the part of at least some men that the feminist slogan, "Women ought not be treated as sex objects" is promulgated only by the puritanical or sexually frigid: "What? She says she doesn't *like* being treated as a sex object? I wish someone would treat *me* that way!"[6] If it is true that the typical case of sex objectification is objectionable, then the expression "sex objectification" will imply treating someone as sexually desirable or stimulating in a *prima facie* inappropriate way which is not entailed by the expression "object of sexual desire" alone.

Furthermore, it is equally misleading to think that what women object to when they complain about being treated as sex objects is that they are being treated as *nothing but* objects of sexual desire. The unhappy wife is considered by her husband to be, among other things, a successful lawyer, and the assistant manager is considered a valuable employee by her boss. Even the free spirit is probably regarded as a source of peer-esteem or a good laugh, as well as sexually attractive. Nevertheless, such women still complain about being treated as sex objects.[7]

To mark out the context in which women are treated as objects of sexual desire appears to be much more helpful. The free spirit is treated as an object of sexual desire in a context where she should be treated as a passerby, but is not. The assistant manager is treated as an object of sexual desire in a context where she should be treated as a business associate. The problem then becomes one of specifying in which contexts persons are inappropriately treated as sexually desirable. However, while the context issue is necessary to understanding the moral offense in the above cases, the case of the unhappy wife shows us that it is not sufficient. For in her case, it is not true that she is being treated as an object of sexual desire in a context where she should be treated as something else. The context is, at least on the surface, appropriate; indeed, treating her as "something else", such as dwelling on her brilliant defense in court that day, might make sex less enjoyable for her than if her husband just treated her as sexy. What we need in our analysis of her case is not only a discussion of the context in which the sexual relations occur, but also the very nature of the relations themselves: the unhappy wife is not being treated as a sex partner in her sexual relations with her husband; she is being treated as a sex *object*.

Just as the complaints against sex objectification are not directed against "sex" *per se,* so too, the complaints against it should not be directed against "objectification" *per se.* There are several examples of circumstances in which persons regard themselves or other persons as things, bodies, parts of bodies, even animals, but which we would not regard as *prima facie* objectionable. Imagine the artist gazing fixedly at the human form he represents on canvas, or imagine the designer of children's clothes hemming a garment draped around the immobile figure of a six-year-old.[8] Imagine the surgeon operating on her patient or the photographer using a face in a crowd (instead of a lamppost or a tree) to focus his camera. Or suppose I shuffle behind a classmate during a ten-year high school reunion to avoid the necessity of conversing with the class gossip. Imagine the kindly uncle playing 'horsey' with his niece, or the anthropologist classifying the members of the species *Homo sapiens* as higher order mammals.

Why do the subjects of the above sorts of treatment fail to complain about their circumstances while the women in our three examples find so much to complain about? One is tempted to say that what distinguishes the former cases from the latter is that the women in our three examples are treated as objects, *but not as persons,*[9] while the artist's model, the surgical patient, the classmate, and so on are treated as objects *but also as persons.* Since objects are insensitive, inanimate things and people are not, treating someone like an object would be to show a disregard for or an indifference to the feelings, desires, or interests that the person in fact has. It would mean treating at least some of the sentiments of a person "as if they did not exist." Clearly the construction workers, husband, and company president show an insensitivity to many of the sentiments of the women they objectify. So the fact that they are not treated as persons would seem to count as the relevant feature in distinguishing their plight from the examples cited just above.

However, closer examination of the ways in which some objects or animals are treated by persons suggests that this distinction has been too hastily drawn. On the one hand, some objects or animals are treated with great care, even affection: witness personal mementoes, gifts from loved ones, prized pets. Indeed, some pet owners treat their pets better than they do other people. Moreover, disregarding some of a person's feelings, desires, or interests "as if they did not exist" may be motivated by a care or concern for the person with those sentiments. For example, suppose that I know you are trying to watch your weight but would love a second helping of dessert. I may not offer you a second helping and so "disregard" or "ignore" what I know to be your desire for seconds out of respect to your own avowed interest in maintaining a trim and healthy body. Yet I can hardly be said to have acted callously or with an insensitivity to your feelings.

Such considerations suggest there is nothing wrong with treating an X as a Y, a rock as a paperweight, an uncle as a brother, Queen Elizabeth as the girl next door, or a person as an object, unless we also stipulate that X is being treated as a Y in ways it should be treated as an X, but is not being so treated. So, for example, it would be inappropriate to treat Queen Elizabeth as the girl next door, if we could show that being Queen Elizabeth carries with it certain rights and requests of us certain attitudes that are violated or rejected when she is treated as the girl next door. Similarly, then, it is not simply that the free spirit, unhappy wife, and assistant manager are being treated as objects and not as persons, or as persons some of whose desires are being disregarded; they are being treated as objects in ways they should be treated as persons, but are not. Furthermore, the situation in which this treatment occurs may itself be inappropriate for sexual encounters, making the moral evaluation of the treatment in such cases one of context as well as one of content.

3. PRECONDITIONS FOR MORAL EQUALITY

In what ways do we treat such things as inanimate objects and non-human animals which are considered inappropriate ways for treating persons? Suppose that we restrict the class of persons to that of human persons, persons that are also human beings. Thus, while some deities or planetary aliens might be referred to as "persons" because of some unique capacity for rational inquiry or moral agency which they possess,[10] the only persons that we shall be concerned with here are biological human beings. My concern is to characterize those features that seem to distinguish mentally fit, fully mature human persons from non-human animals and inanimate objects (including the inanimate or dead human body and its parts). The reason for this concern is that when one has a legitimate claim against persons, that they act toward one in certain ways and not others, and which they are obliged to honor, that claim is a function of the sort of treatment one values or is believed to value from other persons. The more one considers a certain state of physical or psychological well-being to be valuable, for example, the more likely it is that one will demand that others not interfere with the pursuit of that well-being. The less valuable the state, the less likely that any claims to it will either be made or honored. Furthermore, the treatment one values or is believed to value is in turn a function of the capacities to experience oneself and the surrounding world. Thus, if objects and animals have significantly more limited capacities to experience themselves and the world around them, they shall value or be believed to value treatment from persons of a significantly more limited quantitative and qualitative scope. And in turn, they may be said to have significantly more limited claims to (or against) the treatment they receive from persons than persons themselves. We do not always treat objects and animals in ways persons would object to if put in their places. But a person will complain about being treated as an object, specifically, a woman will complain about being treated as a sex object, when she is treated as the kind of thing whose claims on other persons, when compared to their claims on herself and others, are severely restricted or denied altogether.

Just what sorts of claims these are we shall discuss, but it should be understood that these claims are neither exhaustive nor based upon beliefs about the differences between persons and animals or objects that are necessarily or empirically proven true. A claim against an invasion of one's privacy or a claim against rude or uncivil behavior would mean little to those who did not have their claims to adequate food, clothing, and shelter satisfied. Yet it is the former kinds of claims and not the latter that we will discuss.[11] Furthermore, the list that follows of what are typically believed to be distinctively human capacities upon which such rights claims are based does not include many of the capacities traditionally associated with the so-called "feminine" character, such traits as empathy, compassion, intuition, and the capacity to express emotion.[12] Not making direct reference to such traits is specifically not meant to imply that they are either of no importance to persons or believed to be peripheral to what constitutes personhood. The capacities mentioned below were chosen specifically because they explain at least one reason why persons believe certain claims on others' conduct can be legitimately made and honored, and the claims derived from these capacities are the very claims persons most often consider are not honored when they are treated as sex objects. The aim is not to draw a complete picture of what a person is and what claims on others' behavior she or he may legitimately make. Such is the subject of a separate inquiry.[13] The aim is to explain why many persons believe sex objectification is wrong by explaining why persons believe they can legitimately make the specific claims on others' conduct said to be denied in sex objectification.

Furthermore, if the above aim is understood in terms of explaining why persons make the considered judgments about sex objectification that they do, then the so-called "distinctively human capacities" listed below should not be construed as necessarily or empirically proven true; they should be construed only as capacities believed to distinguish persons from other sorts of things. Such beliefs are then used to ground the further belief that certain claims on others' conduct can be made. To imply that such distinctions are in fact true is to imply knowledge about at least certain animals that we do not now possess, or possess only incompletely. Indeed, to imply that we can empirically show that persons have moral rights is the subject of much philosophical debate. [14] In sum, the following is an attempt to explain why persons, women in particular, believe sex objectification is wrong, according to commonly held beliefs about the natures of persons versus those of either animals or objects and, in turn, about the kind of treatment they as persons can claim from others. The extent that such beliefs are true is the extent to which we can validly ground such claims.

A. *Distinctive Human Capacities*

Living persons (hereafter referred to as "persons") have a consciousness or a capacity for sentient life, which allows them not only to feel sensations, but also to have emotions and to entertain moods. Objects such as rocks, typewriters, and neutron stars, at least as far as our own observations tell us, do not. The bodies and body parts of non-living persons (hereafter referred to as "bodies") fall under this object description as well. Furthermore, persons are considered to have a capacity for self-consciousness that no object possesses, and which is typically believed to be of a much more limited sort in non-human animals, if it exists in some of them at all. This capacity entails a capacity for self-awareness and self-criticism. It allows persons to formulate a self-image, viz. some set of characteristics that one takes to be necessary to a picture of oneself; [15] moreover, with such a capacity persons can reflect on their own characters, or observe their own behavior and so attempt to change what they do not like in it. The capacity for self-consciousness is also necessary for persons to feel such things as shame, embarrassment, and humiliation.

So too, persons have a capacity for abstract thought that other animals (and all objects) are believed to lack, the capacity to imagine a wide range of alternative courses of action, to plan for the future, and to predict the future based on what has been previously observed. In this sense, persons are rational, reflective, deliberative beings. In addition, fully mature persons have what are often referred to as "refined sensibilities", that is the moral and aesthetic senses that give them the ability to understand what can count as morally right or wrong conduct and to appreciate and create fine art, literature, and music, as well as the social graces. And finally, in light of their capacity to plan for the future as well as the capacity to reflect on their own actions, fully mature human beings are capable of a degree of self-determination that neither non-human animals nor objects are believed to possess; this capacity includes the ability to develop one's character and the pattern of one's life largely in response to one's own judgments, choices, and personal experience, as opposed to following unreflectively the dictates of one's pre-conditioned or instinctual drives, or to being the subject of the intimidation or psychological domination of other persons.[16]

Let us call the capacities that persons possess but that objects or animals are commonly considered to lack a person's "distinctive human capacities." From the list enumerated above, these capacities include the capacity for sentient life, the capacity for self-awareness, the capacity for abstract thought (including imagination and prediction), a moral sense, an aesthetic sense, and a capacity for self-determination. As mentioned at the close of the previous subsection, I chose to list these specific capacities because, as we shall see, they help explain why it is that persons typically value a level of well-being and freedom in their lives that objects or animals are believed not to value. This does not suggest that persons uniformly value the same level of well-being and freedom; nor does it deny that some persons may value a level of well-being more akin to non-human animals than to persons. The claim is that if persons have capacities to experience themselves and the world around them that are different from those of animals or objects, then those differences can help explain why persons are believed to value a level of well-being and freedom different from that of animals or objects; furthermore, there is a relationship between one's capacities, one's values and one's rights.

B. Capacities, Values, and Rights

An object or body incapable of feeling either physical or psychological distress would not be expected to value the freedom from such suffering that persons typically do. Indeed, without the capacity for consciousness, objects cannot rightly be said to value anything at all. Most mammals are thought to feel at least some kinds of pleasure and pain; but their perceived lack of a more complex psychology is commonly thought to make any satisfaction or discomfort they may feel much narrower in scope than that which persons can feel. Animals are simply not regarded by many as capable of experiencing, much less showing the same emotions that persons do. Thus, they are not believed to value the kind of privacy nor the freedom from certain kinds of embarrassing or humiliating circumstances that persons typically do. (Such beliefs include the speculation that the "ashamed" look of a pet when scolded may be as much anthropomorphism as real shame.)

So too, because of their believed limited capacity for self-awareness, animals seem to be incapable of self-respect, of believing that certain of their own sentiments are worthy of pursuit or satisfaction on their own account, and that they should not be perpetually suppressed or used to others' advantage.[17] Persons may respect the interests, even the rights, if there are any, of animals (see below); but this is quite different from the animal's respect for them. Along similar lines, a non-human animal will be believed to have only a limited, if any, conception of itself as this particular animal among others, of some set of characteristics which it takes to be necessary to any picture of itself. It is persons who are considered capable of valuing and so defending the individuality of their pets, but not the pet themselves, who are believed to have no or a very limited perception of a 'self' to value.

Furthermore, because animals are not believed to have the moral or aesthetic senses that persons do, they are not thought to object to what persons would count as moral or aesthetic "indignities" perpetrated before their eyes; they are not considered to be shocked at the killing of the innocent, or disgusted by lewd conduct, or appreciative of polite manners. Even their ofte.1 lifelong physical confinement or their common and often cruel use by persons for food, experimentation, fashion, or sport are not perceived by the animals (or so we believe) to be the unjust use of themselves or their species. Any moral outrage comes from members of the Humane Society, conservationists, or vegetarians, viz. *persons*. It is not simply that persons do not understand the communications of animals and so do not hear their cries for justice. Many persons simply do not consider animals capable of understanding in any language what an "injustice" is. Also, training an animal for the circus or training it to lead the blind does not seem to run contrary to a nature which is believed to be much more fundamentally motivated than human nature, with its well-developed neo-cortex, by conditioned or instinctual drives. Thus, animals are not believed to value the level of freedom of movement or expression that persons who value the exercise of their self-determination will value.

It seems reasonable to accept the premise that any claims which one makes on others that they treat one in a certain way will typically be claims which one believes will protect what one values.[18] This premise is fostered by the belief that without the ability to make such claims, one would be subject to any treatment from others that they wished, without being able to demand or expect otherwise. One's life would thus be impoverished in so far as one could never be certain that others would allow one to exercise the well-being and freedom one valued. Suppose we call the sort of claim against persons that they treat others in a certain way, and which they are obliged to honor, a "right" to that treatment.[19] Then, if the above premise is true, and if persons can legitimately exercise any rights at all, they will exercise the kinds of rights that insure the well-being and freedom that they value. Without the confidence that they can demand from others a certain freedom from physical and psychological distress and a certain freedom to express themselves and move about as they wish, persons typically regard their lives as both unhappy and unproductive ones.[20]

My claim is that, if we believe objects and animals have rights to well-being and freedom different from those of persons, it is because they are not believed to value the kind of well-being and freedom that persons do. So, for example, since an object is not believed capable of feeling pain, it is not believed capable of valuing freedom from physical discomfort and so be thought to deserve protection from such discomfort by having a claim or right against it. This is not because it cannot "speak" for itself. We often make claims on behalf of children, the infirm, and even the deceased who cannot make their claims good on their own.[21] It is because objects are not the sorts of things that are typically considered capable of valuing anything and so be thought to deserve the sort of treatment from persons which respects what they value. This may well be what is behind the suggestion that objects are not the sorts of things that can have rights.[22] I may refrain from polluting the air because I love the great outdoors or because my children deserve clean air to breathe; but I do not refrain from damaging my physical environment out of a respect for its desire to be free from damage, simply because I believe it has no desires to respect. Entities such as aesthetic objects or objects of our natural environment may require a certain kind of treatment from persons governed by moral rules. But it is my contention, as it is the contention of other philosophers, that any moral rights that involve non-sentient beings are fundamentally rights of *persons* who have an interest in seeing those beings protected, better served, and so on.[23] Indeed, throwing out a good bottle of wine or dismantling a wind-up toy past the point of repair seems to "harm" it only in so far as such actions cause distress to those persons who place some value on the object. The identifying sign of an object, according to one interpretation of Kant's second formulation of the Categorical Imperative ("Do not treat persons merely as means, but always at the same time as ends") is that it has value, whether instrumental or intrinsic, only in so far as some individual other than it assigns value to it. Only persons do not need to be valued either as means or as ends by someone else in order to have value. They are "ends in themselves."[24] For the purpose of this book, the only claims to a certain kind of treatment from persons that objects have will be those claims that have their basis in the interests that persons take in those objects.

Notice that since animals are sentient beings it is a common belief that a good many of them suffer physical (and some psychological) discomfort, and furthermore that they value being free from such discomfort over and above what we might feel at seeing them suffer. Thus, persons tend to agree that many animals do have a claim (indeed the right) to be treated humanely by persons, even if they may have rights to little else.[25] Many persons, for example, feel uneasy about slaughtering cattle that have not been stunned first, or about depriving baby rhesus monkeys of mother-love for purposes of experimentation. Such uneasiness often translates into making claims on behalf of such animals that they be free from a minimum of either physical or psychological distress. Yet many of these same persons do not believe that such creatures can appreciate the value of privacy or can recognize freedom from embarrassment or humiliation in the way that persons do; nor do they believe such animals can value self-respect, a crack wit, a Bach fugue, or polite conversation, when the animals are believed to have no (or a very limited) conception of what such things as privacy, self-respect, or aesthetic satisfaction are. Similarly, it is pointless to ask whether or not they value the freedom from being exploited by persons or the freedom to choose their own life-plans if they cannot understand what their own exploitation or self-determination might be.[26] Thus many persons do not consider animals to have the right to such things as privacy and self-respect, since such persons would not consider animals' lives as in any significant way impoverished without them. Some pet owners may not agree that their pets do not have rights quite similar to those of persons; and some persons may value a kind of well-being and freedom more akin to the typical pet than to human beings. But my aim is only to explain why it is that persons believe they deserve treatment different from animals when they do believe this, and to detail the rights they expect to be honored by others as a consequence.

The fact is that persons can and do feel an acute sense of both physical and psychological distress. They have a sense of who they are as individuals and what interests deserve respect from others. They show a sense of moral outrage at the wrong done others, including the unjust use of persons for others' advantage, as well as the unwarranted invasion of another's privacy. They appreciate aesthetic experience and decry rude or unseemly behavior. And they are able to shape their own lives largely in accordance with their own chosen preferences. As such, persons will typically value a level of well-being and freedom that goes beyond the desires for such basics as food, shelter, and sex which they share with non-human mammals. As a consequence, persons typically will regard their lives as impoverished if they are allowed to enjoy only the level of well-being and freedom that many non-human animals or objects typically enjoy. Moreover, they can be expected to demand the right not only to the basic necessities of human animal survival, but also the kinds of rights to well-being and freedom that protect what they value as persons, and not (merely) as animals or objects.

C. The Rights to Well-Being and Freedom of Persons

From what we have suggested, we can list at least some of the kinds of rights to well-being and freedom that persons typically expect to be able to exercise, and expect others to honor. This list includes those rights that persons would commonly consider objects and animals to enjoy on a much more limited scale than persons do, or not to enjoy at all. It should be emphasized that this list is not meant to be an exhaustive one, but only one that would explain the nature of the complaints made by persons who object to being treated as sex "objects". Furthermore, we shall be concerned here only with the kinds of rights upon which any public system of morality or of the law would be based. This is to distinguish such claims from the kinds of demands made by rules of etiquette or personal taste. Indeed, social convention is not the kind of sphere in which the *right* to correct conduct seems either necessary or appropriate.

To begin our list of rights, then, persons believe they have a right to be free from a reasonable amount of physical injury or suffering. As sentient beings, they believe their physical well-being would be severely diminished without it. Second, they consider a right to privacy important, a right which seems to stem both from a general interest in being free from unwarranted intrusions in their lives and a more specific interest in controlling information persons have about them and observations persons make of them.[27] The paranoia and anxiety which has been documented in those persons deprived of privacy suggests that the lack of it, under certain conditions, is detrimental to their psychological health.[28]

Third, persons feel they have a right to self-respect, to be free from the kind of humiliation that comes from a constant or gratuitous belittling of one's own needs and interests. Fourth, persons expect others not to presume too much about who they are as individuals; they hope that others will take the time, without going so far as to invade their privacy, to appreciate their own point of view on the world and respect the self-image they have created for themselves. Just because I am a mature woman, for example, one need not automatically presume that I am either a housewife or a secretary. This may constitute the ideal situation, as opposed to what persons can demand of others. But I think persons can and do demand that others not arbitrarily classify them as particular sorts of persons when that classification creates an expectation of them that actually prevents them from acting as they would otherwise wish (and when what they wish is no violation of the rights of others or in some way wrong). Recall the human capacity for self-awareness and self-criticism that acts as the prerequisite for valuing such things as privacy, self-respect, and a freedom from stereotyping (for more on stereotyping and role expectations, see Chapter II, section 2B).

Fifth, persons believe they can demand at least civil (as opposed to insulting or gratuitously intrusive) behavior from others; such a belief derives from a general presumption that strangers should be as accommodating as possible, yet nevertheless remain emotionally and physically aloof (the degree of aloofness varying from culture to culture) unless persons expressly desire otherwise or unless the circumstances are socially conducive to increased intimacy. Again, this may be more the ideal than that which persons can demand; but the rules governing "civil" behavior, as merely opposed to the more specific rules of mealtime etiquette, for example, which are a question of convention and taste, seem to have the force of moral prescriptions behind them. Persons' moral sensibilities as well as their aesthetic ones seem to require at least a minimum of decorum or politesse from others to be satisfied.

Sixth, persons demand to be free from the exploitation of others; one feels one has a right to be free from a use by persons which is to their own advantage but at one's own expense.[29] And last, persons demand a level of self-determination in their lives, to be free not only to move about and express themselves without interference, but also to be free to choose their own lifeplans or long-range goals according to preferences they have adopted relatively independently of other persons.[30] Without the capacity or potential to exercise such self-determination, having a right to exercise it would be, practically speaking, meaningless.

Notice that these are rights that are neither unlimited nor absolute; they are rights confined by the competing rights of others and they are rights that may be overridden or waived under special circumstances. So, for example, one does not have a right to an unlimited freedom of movement or expression. One is not free to harm others gratuitously in the pursuit of it. And it may be necessary to restrict persons' freedom of movement, if they do harm others in their pursuit of it, or otherwise abuse the right. Thus, the right to freedom of movement as well as all the rights listed above should be construed as limited *prima facie* rights.[31] In sum, to say that one has a right to a certain sort of treatment from others implies a correlative obligation on the part of those persons over whom the demands of the right extend to refrain from interfering with the exercise of certain capacities or the performance of certain actions as specified by the right. One's right to freedom of movement, for example, is a claim to a certain sort of treatment from others that one can demand in accordance with the specifications of the right.[32] A limited *prima facie* right will be a claim to a certain sort of treatment from others that one can demand only in the face of others' competing rights and which allows special considerations to justify overriding or waiving the right.

4. TREATING WOMEN AS MORAL EQUALS

The rights we have discussed are often labeled "human" rights, since they have their basis in the distinctive human capacities that all persons share. They are also considered equal rights since there is no *prima facie* rationale for making distinctions among persons whose capacities to experience, and so to value a certain level of well-being and freedom, are approximately the same.[33] However, for those of special need or merit, an extraordinary share in the distribution of valued goods and services may be justified as long as such inequalities can be justified on the same grounds as those which justify the original position of equality.[34] The same conditions for justifying inequalities apply to those persons who would justify overriding the rights of others or those who would voluntarily waive their rights (see Chapter II, section 3).

Let us stipulate, using symbols, that A is the "moral equal" of persons when A has the basic human rights to well-being and freedom listed above equal to those of any other person.[35] For a woman to be treated as a moral equal by persons, then, especially when those persons are men, will entail two conditions: (1) the woman so treated is conceived of (by those persons) as a moral equal, that is a person who has the human rights to well-being and freedom equal to those of any other person; and (2) she is acted toward (by those persons) in ways that do not violate those rights. Persons who treat women as moral equals believe that women are deserving of a happy, relatively unencumbered life. Such persons do not wish to dominate the lives of women or control the interests of women. They do not coerce, harm, humiliate, or oppress women in a way that violates women's human rights to well-being and freedom.

Given the stipulation above, those women who value a certain level of well-being and freedom in their lives, a level guaranteed by their human rights to well-being and freedom, can legitimately demand the *prima facie* right to be treated as the moral equals of other persons. At least, we can say that women (and persons generally) have a right to be acted toward as moral equals. That is, they can demand that others accord them the kind of well-being and freedom guaranteed by their human rights. However, notice that to *treat* someone as a moral equal may mean either conceiving of that person as a moral equal or acting in a way which is not in violation of her or his rights to well-being and freedom, or both. I offer the more limited claim about acting toward one as a moral equal above, because it seems too restrictive of other persons' rights to demand that they not *think* about us in a certain way, even though we do talk about rights against persons for their *conduct* toward us. How would one go about insuring that the right was not violated? (Lie detectors? Brain waves?) And how much is that demand an invasion of one's own right to privacy? Certainly one would want to prohibit the cultivation of those attitudes that tend to motivate or engender undesirable behavior. When persons worry about how others think about them, they are often concerned only with how much of what is thought about them will actually affect them. So, for example, women have been known to object to pornography on the grounds that it puts sadistic thoughts in men's heads which lead them to sadistic action.[36] But others simply object to the view of women (as sexual slaves, pets, or whipping girls) that is portrayed by some pornographic material.[37] The idea is that anyone who conceives of women in this way entertains an objectionable or inappropriate attitude toward women, whatever that person's overt actions toward women may be.

In fact, while we may not be able to demand that we be thought about in a certain way, we often find some attitudes objectionable and others not, even when the behavior of the person entertaining the attitudes appears impeccable. For example, a man with fantasies of raping women may act toward them in a morally unobjectionable way only because he was somehow prevented from acting inappropriately when intending to do otherwise. Often we censure persons whose overt conduct appears appropriate but who laugh inwardly at the misfortunes of others, or who secretly carry a grudge against anyone who makes friends easily, or who have an especially spiteful or envious nature. So there is nothing new in thinking that attitudes or motives can be inappropriate even if they find no outlet in practice. We simply tend to say the person has a less than virtuous character, rather than say that person has violated anyone's rights.

In any case, it seems to me that whether or not we women have a right to a certain conception of ourselves as moral equals, to conceive of ourselves as anything less is a *prima facie* inappropriate attitude to take. The suggestion is that it is not enough that men simply refrain from acting toward women in ways that violate their rights to well-being and freedom. Men are expected to have the proper attitude toward women as well. Persons generally object to any other person who thinks of them as fundamentally undeserving of the kind of well-being and freedom that others have, even if such a person may never lift a finger to deprive them of that condition. And they often demand that the person come around to a different way of thinking. Moreover, even if persons are not aware that negative attitudes toward them are entertained by any other person, they not only act on the assumption that such a person *does* think of them as moral equals, but they also believe such a person *should* think of them in that way. For example, black persons typically demand that whites do more than grudgingly accord them their human rights to well-being and freedom: they want white men and women to think of them as persons deserving of those rights.[38] Any person who conceives of women as less than moral equals has a *prima facie* inappropriate attitude, even though no inappropriate behavior may accompany it or be motivated by it, and even though such attitudes are probably the ideal and not the right of persons.

5. TREATING WOMEN AS SEX OBJECTS: TREATING WOMEN AS LESS THAN MORAL EQUALS

The more we treat toys or pets as if they valued (and so deserved) the level of well-being and freedom that persons do, the more we may be said to be treating those things as if they were persons. Conversely, one way to treat a person as an object is to treat her or him as if she or he lacked the rights or the scope of the rights to well-being and freedom that persons have.

Thus, one way in which we can explain why the artist's model might not mind being treated "as an object" is that the model is being treated as if she were an object (a stationary mass, a figurine, a body) but also as a moral equal: she is a person with a body that is useful for creating figures in oil paintings, and who is both regarded as the bearer of the human rights to well-being and freedom equal to those of other persons and acted toward in a way which is not in violation of those rights.

In the ideal case, for example, she is neither coerced nor humiliated into standing erect or changing positions on demand. Moreover, she has full control over how much of her body she wants others to observe. She is not being exploited by being deceived about the payment she shall receive or about what is expected of her while on the job. We can suppose the artist is neither rude to her nor attempts to become too intimate in the face of any of the model's clear desires to the contrary. In fact, as far as we can tell, he may presume that she is only interested in business as usual. He does not try to subordinate her interests to his; we can imagine that she chooses to model out of her own personal preference, finding a great deal of personal satisfaction in helping an artist create a beautiful work of art.

On the other hand, the well-being and freedom of the three women in our examples of sex objectification have been severely diminished by their objectifiers. The free spirit feels embarrassed by the fact that her more "private" parts are now the subject of public discussion and a kind of disconcerting curiosity by persons she does not even know. She wonders how many men have been "checking her out" without her knowing it. Some anxiety, even some paranoia over the thought of such constant public scrutiny begins to set in. She is frightened by the thought that men have been known to rape women with no provocation. She finds the behavior of the workers a rude intrusion on her daily routine; in fact, she feels she can no longer walk freely and unselfconsciously down her own street in broad daylight. As far as she is concerned, her rights to privacy, freedom of movement and expression, and to at least civil behavior from the construction workers have been violated in this context.

The unhappy wife begins to wonder where the intimacy in her sexual relationship with her husband has gone. His insensitivity to her own feelings about sex makes her wonder whether he ever tries to look at sex from her point of view. In fact, if she had not overheard him bragging about her brilliant legal defense, she would wonder just what else she means to him besides a "quick lay." Because her husband refuses to think that her own sexual needs have any real bearing on her happiness at all, she begins to wonder herself just how important those needs really are. Thus, a certain degree of her own self-respect diminishes. She need not feel this way; the point is that it is easy for her to feel this way, given the dominating and controlling attitude of her husband.

The assistant manager fumes at the fact that her boss has exploited the power relationship that exists between them to try to convince her to go to bed with him. She feels unfairly used by him for an easy turn-on; she is disgusted by his self-display and feels that brain or no brain, she is ultimately a sexual tool for his own personal purposes, without really considering her purposes. The offer of sex in exchange for promotion intimidates her, since she feels she cannot refuse without leaving the company, yet she does not wish to submit. Thus, she feels a certain lack of freedom to pursue her own sex life (and career) in the way that she would otherwise wish. She also finds it presumptuous of her boss to think that she would be happy to "mix a little business with pleasure."

The attitudes of the sex objectifiers are those of confidence, domination, and control. The construction workers see their machismo reaffirmed by displaying themselves to the free spirit as sexually confident initiators of their encounter. They know they can make her feel embarrassed and use her embarrassment as a source of amusement. The husband believes his sexual interests should dominate those of his wife, and he feels confident that she will submit to his demands once she recognizes what he regards as their validity. The company president imposes his will on the assistant manager, not so much by forcing her to have sex with him as by making it difficult for her to choose otherwise. He sees her potential for the office, but wants to be sure he gets his own personal satisfaction from her as well. And his power position is a resource for that end.

A central theme of our examples would seem to be the subjugation, subordination, intimidation or psychological domination of the sex object.[39] Such a theme is consistent with the claim that the sex objectifier treats the sex object as less than a moral equal, as one less deserving, not equally so, of the rights to well-being and freedom that he enjoys. Notice that the willingness to dominate the interests of another, to humiliate, threaten, or otherwise constrain the freedom of another seems to typify the attitude of men like the construction workers, husband, and company president. They all show an attitude that conceives of women as less than moral equals. The free spirit is considered to be "a nice piece of ass." The unhappy wife sees herself, through the eyes of her husband, as "a sexually stimulating machine." The assistant manager regards her position as one of "a sexual servant" or "an appreciative pet." They react strongly and negatively to the fact that they are treated as the sexual toys, tools, props, or pets of the men with whom they come in contact. But as the case of the artist's model suggests, being treated as an object, body, or animal is not the whole story. Nor is it necessary that the sex object react or even react negatively to her sex objectification (we shall investigate such alternatives in Chapter II). What is necessary to identify an incident as sex objectification is that the sex object be treated as an object, body, or animal but not also as the moral equal of persons. She is treated as if she lacked one or more of the distinctive human capacities upon which her rights to a certain level of well-being and freedom are based. She is treated as if she were the sort of creature who had no such rights or rights of a very limited sort. This is equivalent to saying that with respect to her rights to well-being and freedom, she is treated in the very way she would commonly be treated, if she were an animal, body, or object.

Given the thesis that the sex object is treated as less than a moral equal by her objectifier, we can explain the pervasive complaint that sex objectification degrades women or demeans women. The sex object is a moral inferior or moral subordinate; she literally has been lowered in status not merely from that of person to object, but from that of moral equal to moral subordinate. She is treated as if she were the sort of being with more restricted rights, less of the rights, or none of the rights to well-being and freedom that other persons (in particular, her objectifiers) enjoy. Some or all of the sex object's feelings, desires, or interests are subordinated, subverted, and manipulated to satisfy the sex objectifier's own, in a *prima facie* inappropriate way. We shall call such degradation or subordination "dehumanization" to distinguish it from the simple "objectification" of the artist's model in our example. What this analysis suggests is that one can treat a woman as sexually attractive without treating her as a sex object, by treating her as a sexually attractive moral equal or person. This suggestion matches the intuition of at least some people that while a woman may be complimented for her sexy body, or regarded as an erotic bedmate, she need not automatically be construed as a sex object.[40] In short, a person is dehumanized when that person is treated as an animal, body, part of body, or object in ways she or he should be treated as a person, that is as a moral equal. The woman who is treated as a sex object is a woman dehumanized.

6. ON DEHUMANIZATION

Before we give a complete preliminary characterization of sex objectification, we should examine this notion of the dehumanization of persons in a bit more detail.

First, dehumanization need not be confined to the area of sexual relations. Human slavery is often called a dehumanizing practice, for example. The Negro slave of nineteenth century America was shackled, beaten, and forced to work long hours as if she or he had no right to her or his own physical freedom. Any interests in pursuing a life of her or his own were subordinated in favor of the fiscal interests of the slavemaster. The industrial factory can promote dehumanizing conditions as well, by providing little or no outlet for its workers to participate in the policy decisions of its company. They cannot determine the conditions of their labor, and if the tasks are repetitive or mundane under such conditions, the workers cannot exercise any kind of freedom of expression or enjoy any sort of personal satisfaction in their work. They become like so many pre-programmed machines. The inmates of prison camps who are denied all privacy or intimacy among themselves are victims of dehumanizing conditions as well. Under such conditions, they are treated similarly to those animals who cannot or do not value such things as a private moment alone or an intimate conversation and so are not accorded rights to protect them. So too, inmates are often beaten or starved by guards who see them as so many toys for their amusement. These are persons who are treated as animals or objects but not also as moral equals, i.e. treated as the sorts of things which have little or no rights to the kind of well-being and freedom that other persons enjoy.

Second, it is only in certain respects that the persons dehumanized above are treated like objects or animals. They are starved or made to feel pain, and they can feel humiliation and appreciate the poverty of their condition. However, real animals are considered by many to be unable to feel the kind of humiliation that persons do, and real objects cannot be starved or feel pain or value creating their own working environments. Those respects in which the persons above are treated as less than human, then, are those respects in which their rights to well-being and freedom as human beings or persons have been violated or otherwise abused. They are not treated in all respects, or even in many respects, like objects.

So too, the construction worker who considers the free spirit a "nice piece of ass" does not reduce her to her ass or think her ass in some way represents her, as some authors have thought.[41] What he reduces her to is the sort of thing which he can treat as his moral subordinate, the sort of thing he can subjugate or dominate or control. He can make her feel uncomfortable; he can force her to take a different route home from school. He treats her as if she were some "piece of ass" only in so far as he sees her as a sexually attractive person who can (or should) be degraded to the status of something without the rights to well-being and freedom that persons have. A woman's buttocks, taken by themselves, are just such things.

Similarly, the husband may act as if all he wants is a sexually stimulating machine, but it is the sexual domination over the person of his wife, and not that of a programmable machine, that makes their sex enjoyable for him. So too, the company president does not regard his choice of sex partner as that of some simple pet parakeet or cocker spaniel, but of an intelligent businesswoman whose position in the company can be used to extract sexual favors. The sex objectifier is not someone, as some have claimed, who wants sex with a real thing, body, or animal and so treats women exactly as if they were such things. The real picture is much more complicated. The term "object" in "sex object" does not carry its usual connotations, but is synonymous with the term "subordinate" or the expression "object but not also moral equal." The woman who is treated as a sex object is a person degraded from the status of moral equal to the sort of thing which is considered unequal or inferior to other persons with respect to their human rights to well-being and freedom. Thus, the sex "object" is treated as an animal, body, or object with respect to her rights to well-being and freedom; she is not literally treated in all respects like an object. This common misunderstanding explains why the male sex objectifier is apt to say, "I'm not treating her like an object. I wouldn't whistle at her if she weren't a girl!" Such a remark is consistent with Simone deBeauvoir's claim that women are in an "ambiguous situation . . . as object paradoxically embued with subjectivity."[42] As persons, women are the moral equals (her "subjects") of other persons, thus in a morally legitimate position to act autonomously in the world. But because they are women, they are defined as Other, as object or thing, "inferior and inessential"[43], by men considered the defining "subjects" of contemporary western culture. According to this view, if women are treated as sexually desirable in so many contexts where that treatment is otherwise inappropriate, indeed "sexualized" by the culture, it is because they are defined *by men* in terms of their sexual attractiveness *to men*.[44] Thus women are made into the Kantian objects we mentioned in section 3B by having value in the culture only in so far as those other than themselves place value on them.

Moreover, looking at examples of dehumanization in spheres outside the sexual one suggests that the dehumanization of a person can be of distinct types. The person born into slavery may literally lose much of his ability to live a life independently of the dictates of his master; the prison inmate may be given enough drugs to forget who or where he is. Such examples are quite different from those in which the slave or inmates retain their distinctive human capacities, but are simply kept from exercising them. Such observations suggest we must consider at least two forms of dehumanization: (1) causing a person to be an object in a way that fails to treat that person as a moral equal; and (2) treating a person as if she or he were an object in a way that fails to treat that person as a moral equal. The distinction between (1) and (2) is actually a distinction between forms of objectification. These two categories help us answer the question: In what ways can a person treat a person as an object?

First, for a person to cause another person to be an animal, body, or object involves manipulating the circumstances in which that person lives in such a way that the person is either prevented from developing some or all of her or his distinctive human capacities or is caused to lose some such capacity already developed. In other words, that person is effectively reduced to realizing only those capacities that things, bodies, or animals have. Thus one can beat others to the point of irrationality, or drug or hypnotize persons so that they are no longer self-aware or self-determining. Starvation or long periods of physical confinement have similar effects. Children who have been abused all their lives by their parents often do not fully develop their capacities for rationality or self-determination; and the child locked in the basement by a vicious guardian can hardly be expected to develop any sort of aesthetic sensibilities when she or he is having to concentrate merely on survival.

Not all objectification is *dehumanizing,* a claim consistent with my contention that treating a person as an object is not always or only to treat her or him as less than a moral equal. Hypnotism may be used to cure debilitating neuroses, and drugs that initially cloud the mind can be used to achieve both good health and, ultimately, a clear head. The point is that such causal objectification becomes causal dehumanization when the person *qua* object is unjustifiably treated as deserving less of the kind of well-being and freedom that other persons enjoy. Thus hypnotism that is performed to cure the neurosis of a patient who has voluntarily and with full knowledge consented to undergo it is not dehumanization; but hypnotism without informed consent or with the intent of creating an army of obedient automatons does count as dehumanization.

Notice that this sort of "causal" dehumanization is conspicuously absent from the three examples of sex objectification we have offered. It is seldom true that the sex objectifier literally causes the object of his attentions to lose one of her human capacities. As we noted earlier in this section, part of her sexual attraction is in her full humanity. However, the violent husband or rapist could conceivably beat or drug his object in such a way that he would cause such a person to be little more than an animal or object with respect to her human capacities. On the other hand, even rape need not be construed as causal dehumanization in the sense above. One might also be treated merely *as if* one were a kind of sexual instrument but not also as a moral equal with a right against bodily harm. We shall review this general form of dehumanization below; in any case, we should mention here that rape, particularly the rape of women, is not unequivocally viewed as a kind of *sex* objectification at all, since many consider rape to be a crime of assault and not a crime of an attempted satisfaction of a sexual need.[45]

We actually have already characterized what I shall call "hypothetical" dehumanization, versus the "causal" dehumanization above, when we introduced the reasons for the sex object's complaints at the beginning of section 5. First, we need to explicate the sort of objectification involved in this second sort of dehumanization. A woman is treated *as if* she were an object when the treatment she receives from others is the same sort of treatment she would receive if she were an object. Such a person is not caused to lose any of her human capacities, only treated in ways similar to those things that lack human capacities. In this respect, one might argue that causal dehumanization is a far more damaging form of dehumanization than one which, while treating one like an object, does not make one into an object. Nevertheless, like causing a person to be an object, one may be treated as if one were an object in quite an unobjectionable fashion. Some mannequins are used to size clothes; some models are used to size clothes. Some horses are ridden by children; some kindly uncles are ridden by children. A woman is hypothetically dehumanized when the treatment she receives is the same sort of treatment she would get if she were an object, but not also the moral equal of other persons. Such a woman is treated as if she lacked some or all of the distinctive human capacities upon which her rights to well-being and freedom are based. With respect to such rights, she is being treated in the very way an object or animal is typically treated. This is just the position of the free spirit, the unhappy wife, and assistant manager. Their complaints about being treated as sex objects are complaints about being treated as if they were the sorts of things without the rights to well-being and freedom that persons in fact have.

We can analyze sex objectification, then, as one of two types of dehumanization within the context of persons' sexual relations with one another. The context of such relations is simply the context of persons' sexual admiration, attraction, stimulation, or satisfaction by themselves or other persons. Thus, for example, two persons[46] are engaged in sexual relations with one another on this model when they are engaged in sexual intercourse, orgasm, foreplay, or petting; but they are also engaged in such relations when one or the other or both persons find the other person sexually admirable or attractive without the paradigmatic bodily contact that so often constitutes such relations. In other words, it is sufficient for two persons to be engaged in sexual relations with one another if one person is the object of some sort of psycho-physiological response in the other person, associated with the arousal of some or all of that person's genital parts or organs.[47] The relations may be reciprocal or one-sided; and in particular, as we have suggested above, the encounter may never culminate in any physical contact, much less sexual intercourse or foreplay culminating in orgasm. The person doing the attracting or providing the stimulation need not even be aware that she or he is the object of such a response in someone else. The point is to characterize such relations sufficiently loosely in order to capture any personal encounter in which one person is sexually attractive to another (or to oneself, see Chapter II, section 3A), where that attraction is an essential element to a complete description of the encounter.

7. A PRELIMINARY CHARACTERIZATION OF SEX OBJECTIFICATION

Let us then characterize sex objectification as follows: person A treats person B as a sex object, or A engages in the sex objectification of B if and only if three conditions hold: (1) A dehumanizes B in some context C of A's sexual relations with B; A's dehumanization of B in C implies that A either causes B to be like an object or treats B as if B were an object in a way that violates or rejects in a *prima facie* inappropriate manner one or more of B's rights to well-being and freedom in C; (2) A values B in C solely or primarily in terms of B's instrumental ability to sexually attract, stimulate, or satisfy A; and (3) B's ability to sexually attract A as described in (2) is both the source and the means for A's dehumanization of B described in (1).

Some explanation of the phrasing of the characterization is in order. First, both A and B are persons whose sex remains unspecified. Although the paradigm cases in this chapter have been those of women who are treated as sex objects by men, Chapter II includes a discussion of the sex objectification of men by women and the sex objectification of homosexuals (and heterosexuals) by other homosexuals. Second, the characterization sets out three conditions, individually necessary and jointly sufficient for treating a person as a sex object. The first condition states that the sex objectifier treats the sex object as less than a moral equal in some context of their sexual relations. It was argued earlier in this chapter that the feature of moral equality distinguishes the objectionable from unobjectionable cases of treating a person as an object. Furthermore, it is the feature that distinguishes treating a person as a sex object from merely treating a person as sexy. The second condition states that the sex object's ability to attract the objectifier sexually should count as the primary or sole source of the sex object's worth or value to the objectifier in that context. And third, the sex object's ability to attract the objectifier is both the source and the vehicle or means for the sex object's dehumanization.

The fact that A finds B sexually attractive not only provides a context for B's dehumanization, but that sexuality becomes a kind of focus for her humiliation, embarrassment, and domination. So, for example, A may consciously want to subordinate B and so use sex in order to do so. The husband of the unhappy wife seems to fulfill his desire to dominate her in this way, and we can imagine the company president wanting to exercise a kind of power over the assistant manager by seeking to extract sexual favors for her promotion. On the other hand, A may dehumanize B simply in the way A responds to B's sexuality, without consciously intending to use sex as such a vehicle. The free spirit was not necessarily the object of the kind of purposeful domination noted above, although this may have been true, or at least partly so. (See the account of sexism, Chapter II, section 2). In either case, B is treated as sexually attractive, but in way which is comparable to being treated as a sexual instrument and not a moral equal. A fails to treat B (the sex object) as a moral equal when B's sexual attractiveness is considered by A to be a feature of her personality which can appropriately be used to deny her some or all of the rights to well-being and freedom that A enjoys. Thus B's sexuality is both the source and instrument through which her dehumanization takes place.

Notice that it is not simply that A finds B sexy and also treats B as less than a moral equal. The slave can be thought of by her master both as sexually stimulating and as no more deserving of freedom than his plowhorse, but he is not thereby treating her as a sex object. The dehumanization of the sex object is an integral feature of the sexual relations between A and B, not something conjoined to those relations, logically independent of them. However, it is also not the case that A treats B as less than a moral equal *because* B is sexy. A may treat some persons that A finds sexually attractive as sex objects, but not treat others that way. A treats B as a sex object when B's sexuality is treated both as the source of her dehumanization and the instrument for it. Her sexuality may not be treated in this manner, but then B would not be treated as a sex object.

Furthermore, the characterization of sex objectification stipulates that it occur "in some context C" of A's sexual relations with B. This expression is used to capture such cases as the unhappy wife, who had some enjoyable sex with her husband at one point in their marriage and unenjoyable sex only when he got drunk. Also, it places the instrumental sexual value which A sees in B squarely within the context of A's sexual relations with B. The unhappy wife is also valued by her husband as an able lawyer, but in the context (or some context) of her sexual relations with him, that value is replaced by that of sexual stimulant or satisfier.

However, even within the context of those relations, the sex object's value may be only primarily, not solely, placed in her ability to turn A on. B may also be valued in that context as a source of self-esteem, a good laugh, as a diligent employee, a subordinate wife, and so on. Her value as a sexual stimulant is of primary importance, certainly; and as in the case of the assistant manager or *Playboy* centerfold photo captioned with a list of the subject's career interests, the sex object's more cerebral merits may be subsumed under how sexy she seems to others. Nevertheless, it is misleading to suggest, as some authors have done, that what is true of sex objectification is that only one aspect of the sex object is valued, namely her capacity as a sexual turn-on.[48] The fact that the unhappy wife is valued as a competent lawyer by her husband is a typical counterexample to this claim; furthermore, we can find counterexamples even when we have specified the context in which the sex objectification occurs. The assistant manager is valued both as an efficient businesswoman and as a sexual prize in the circumstances in which her sex objectification occurs. But even if B's ability to stimulate others is taken to be B's sole merit in a given context, that merit is valued by A in an objectionable way only when it implies that A gives *prima facie* insufficiently appropriate consideration to B's well-being and freedom.

Given such examples as the assistant manager and career-oriented *Playboy* bunny above, the characterization of sex objectification stipulates that it is 'B' and not 'B's body' or 'B's body parts' that can do the stimulating. B can be a sex object with a sexy personality, manner or intellect. The fact that she is a sex object and not a sexually stimulating person lies in the fact that she is treated as a sexual subordinate by her objectifier. She may be "just a body" to those who do not know her better; but appreciating her intelligence is no barrier to treating her as a sex object.

Also notice that the sex object's value is in her "instrumental" ability to excite her objectifier. This term is used to emphasize two points: (1) that B is treated as a Kantian object whose value lies not in her own estimation of herself but in the value A places on her as the instrument of his own enjoyment, power, status, etc.; and (2) that B is not treated as an aesthetic object, not enjoyed for her own sake, but used for some (instrumental) purpose which the observer has beyond that enjoyment. Neither claim is meant to suggest that the sex object's dehumanization lies merely in her being "used" by her objectifier. Persons are used to deliver messages and hold ladders without moral censure. The use to which the sex object is put is a *prima facie* objectionable use which involves treating her as less than a moral equal. Furthermore, the latter claim is meant to point out that a sex object is not regarded in the way the Venus de Milo or a Botticelli nude is regarded. The sex object is a sexual instrument valued for its ability to turn others on. Perhaps this is why it is so easy a transition from sexual instrument to sex object. A woman, like a sculpture, may be beautiful or inspired, but only a sexual instrument gets labeled "a nice piece of ass."[49]

One can be more or less successful as treating another person as a sex object in so far as one is more or less successful at using sex as the vehicle for either (1) formulating a conception of a person as deserving less or none of the human rights to well-being and freedom that other persons enjoy, listed in the formulation of sex objectification above under "rejecting" those rights, or (2) interfering with the thoughts and/or actions of a person in such a way that it violates those rights. The important point to note so far is that the sex object is treated as a sexual subordinate, not as a moral equal. Some or all of the sex object's sentiments are subordinated to the objectifier's own in a *prima facie* inappropriate way. And the sex object's rights to well-being and freedom are treated as limited or non-existent. This interpretation helps explain why the women in our examples complain about being treated as sex objects, given the fact that objects are not always treated in ways persons find objectionable; and it can explain much of the specific content of those complaints as well. The sex object is degraded from the status of person with certain rights to well-being and freedom to that of animal, body, or object with little or no such rights at all. In this way, she is treated as an object when she should be treated as a person.

NOTES

1 For examples, *see* Chapter II, section 3.

2 The term "inappropriate" is used here and throughout the book with regard to sex objectification to signify some form of moral indictment, either against those sex-objectifying actions that violate some moral right or rights of the sex objects or against those attitudes of the sex objectifier which, while not in and of themselves injustices for which one is morally entitled to redress, nevertheless invite moral reprobation of some sort. For more on the morality of sex objectifying attitudes versus actions, *see* Chapter I, section 4.

3 For a clear and succinct account of the notion of "*prima facie*" in terms of *prima facie* rights, *see* Gregory Vlastos, "Justice and Equality" in *Social Justice,* ed. Richard B. Brandt (Englewood Cliffs, New Jersey: Prentice-Hall, 1962), p. 38, footnote 23.

4 *See* John Barth, *Giles Goat Boy* (New York: Fawcett World Library, 1974), p. 235.

5 Elizabeth Eames, "Sexism and Woman as Sex Object," *Journal of Thought* 11, No. 2 (April, 1976), p. 142.

6 *See* Robert Baker, " 'Pricks' and 'Chicks': A Plea for Persons" in *Philosophy and Sex,* ed. Robert Baker and Frederick Elliston (Buffalo, New York: Prometheus Books, 1975), p. 55. *Also see* my discussion of the male sex object, *infra* Chapter II, section 4 where I describe those cases of men who might enjoy their purported sex objectification by women and those who do not.

7 *See* Baker, *op. cit.,* p. 55; *also see* my criticisms of Baker on this point, *infra* Chapter III, section 3. Furthermore, while it may be true that women in general are defined largely, and often solely, in terms of the sexual, it is the fact that they are defined *by men* in terms of their sexual attraction *to men,* a definition they largely adopt for themselves, that crystallizes the meaning of "objectification" in "sex objectification." *See infra* Chapter I, section 6 and Chapter II, section 2B.

8 *See* Norvin Richards, "Using People," *Mind* 87, No. 345 (January, 1978), p. 102. Richards uses the example of a designer and fashion model. However, since some women find modelling an instance of, or at least contributing to a climate of sex objectification, I have used a less controversial example.

9 *See* Eames, *op. cit.,* p. 141.

10 For an account of persons as uniquely rational and (thereby) moral agents, *see* Immanuel Kant, *Groundwork of the Metaphysics of Morals,* trans. H. J. Paton (New York: Harper Torchbooks, Harper & Row, 1964), pp. 61ff. For the way in which conceiving of persons as moral agents may be used in an analysis of abortion, *see* Michael Tooley, "A Defense of Abortion and Infanticide" in *The Problem of Abortion,* ed. Joel Feinberg (Belmont, California: Wadsworth Publishing Company, 1973), pp. 54ff.

11 I thank Mary Vetterling-Braggin for pointing this out to me, as well as for the concerns about a male-biased rights list mentioned below.

12 For a list of these traits, *see* e.g. Joyce Trebilcot, "Two Forms of Androgynism" and Mary Anne Warren, "Is Androgyny the Answer to Sex Stereotyping?" in *"Femininity," "Masculinity," and "Androgyny",* ed. Mary Vetterling-Braggin (Totowa, New Jersey: Littlefield, Adams & Co., 1982).

13 *See,* e.g. Mary Anne Warren, "On the Moral and Legal Status of Abortion" in *Philosophy and Women,* ed. Sharon Bishop and Marjorie Weinzweig, (Belmont, California: Wadsworth Publishing Co., 1974); Jane English, "Abortion and the Concept of a Person" in *Feminism and Philosophy,* ed. Mary Vetterling-Braggin, Frederick A. Elliston, and Jane English (Totowa, New Jersey: Littlefield, Adams & Co., 1978); and David Lyons, ed., *Rights* (Belmont, California: Wadsworth Publishing Co., 1979).

14 *See,* e.g. Joel Feinberg, "The Nature and Value of Rights" in Lyons, *op. cit.*

15 For an analysis of the nature and importance of this self-conception in persons, *see* Bernard Williams, "The Idea of Equality" in his *Problems of the Self: Philosophical Papers 1956-1972* (London: Cambridge University Press, 1973), pp. 236-237. *Also see* Elizabeth Spelman, "Treating Persons as Persons," *Ethics* 88, No. 2 (January, 1978), pp. 150-161.

16 To the extent that our instinctual drives, genetic determinants, and so on determine our own behavior, we cannot call ourselves "self-determined." However, if we are self-determined at all, it is typically argued that we are not motivated solely or even primarily by such factors as perhaps non-human animals are. That animals do not have the capacity for self-determination is argued in Michael Fox, " 'Animal Liberation': A Critique," *Ethics* 88, No. 2 (January, 1978), pp. 106ff. For more on self-determination in the absence of intimidation or indoctrination, *see* Sharon Bishop Hill, "Self-Determination and Autonomy" in Bishop and Weinzweig, *op. cit.,* pp. 68-77.

17 *See* Thomas E. Hill, Jr., "Servility and Self-Respect" in *Today's Moral Problems,* ed. Richard Wasserstrom (New York: Macmillan Publishing Company, 1975), pp. 136-152.

18 *See* Richard Wasserstrom, "Rights, Human Rights, and Racial Discrimination" in Lyons, *op. cit.,* p. 53.

19 *See* Joel Feinberg, "The Nature and Value of Rights" in Lyons, *op. cit.*, pp. 78–91.

20 *See* Vlastos, in Brandt, *op. cit.*, pp. 49ff.

21 *See* Joel Feinberg, "The Rights of Animals and Unborn Generations" in *Today's Moral Problems*, 2nd ed., ed. Richard Wasserstrom (New York: Macmillan Publishing Company, 1979), pp. 584ff.

22 Feinberg's suggestion is that since objects do not have cognitive beliefs and desires, they cannot have the kinds of "interests" that are protected by rights. *See Ibid.*, pp. 582ff.

23 For an especially clear example of how a person's aesthetic interest can determine or guide how we treat the objects of that interest, *see* Mark Sagoff, "On Preserving the Natural Environment," in Wasserstrom, 2nd ed., *op. cit.*, pp. 613–622.

24 For this interpretation of Kant, *see* Vlastos, *op. cit.*, p. 49.

25 For an analysis of the sorts of rights that animals may have, *see* Lawrence Haworth, "Rights, Wrongs, and Animals," *Ethics* 88, No. 2 (January, 1978), pp. 95–105. For some arguments against the claim that animals can have rights at all, *see* Michael Fox, *op. cit.*, pp. 106–118. The fact that we do not accuse the fly-swatter or the fishmonger of "inhumane" treatment when they smack or hook or suffocate their prey could be because we simply do not believe that such animals have the cognitive sensations of pain and pleasure that mammals do. Perhaps it is because human beings are also mammals and have a certain bias toward, or ability to empathize with, animals of their own kind, or it may simply be because such animals do not appear or act as if they feel pain. Inhibiting the spontaneous movement of a gnat can be accomplished with as much indifference to any of its pleasures or pains as dismantling a wind-up toy. Compare this indifference to the empathy we have toward the cocker spaniel who, when hurt, goes limping about, whimpering, and generally casting (what appears to be) a doleful eye on all around it. This latter claim might lead one to think that some animals appear more like the "innocent victim" to human beings than some others, a belief perhaps grounded in the human ability to empathize with certain animals and not others we noticed earlier. A rabbit, for example, may have little in common physiologically with a human being, but can conjure up feelings of warmth, helplessness, or victimization that a mosquito or barracuda cannot.

26 One rationale for the master-slave relationship in any culture has been that the slave does not understand what freedom is; thus, according to the master, the slave can neither miss it nor would she know what to do with it, if she had it.

27 For a review of some of the recent philosophical literature on privacy, *see* Jeffrey H. Reiman, "Privacy, Intimacy, and Personhood," *Philosophy and Public Affairs* 6, No. 1 (Fall, 1976), pp. 26–44. For a general outline of the problems associated with losing one's privacy, *see* Richard Wasserstrom, "Privacy; Some Arguments and Assumptions" in *Philosophical Law: Authority, Equality, Adjudication, Privacy*, ed. Richard Bronaugh (Westport, Connecticut: Greenwood Press, 1978).

28 *See* Erving Goffman, *Asylums* (Hawthorne, New York: Aldine Publishing Company, 1961), pp. 23–25.

29 For an account of exploitation, *see* Judith Tormey, "Exploitation, Oppression and Self-Sacrifice" in *Women and Philosophy*, ed. Carol C. Gould and Marx W. Wartofsky (New York: G. P. Putnam's Sons, 1976), pp. 206–215. *Also see* Joel Feinberg, "Consenting to Exploitation," unpublished manuscript, July, 1980. And *see* my account of the exploitation of women in pornography, *infra*, Chapter III, section 1.

30 Whether or not this kind of autonomy is possible in a society with well-defined sex roles is taken up by Richard Wasserstrom in "Racism and Sexism" in his *Philosophy and Social Issues* (Notre Dame, Indiana: University of Notre Dame Press, 1980), pp. 40ff. *Also see* Robert Young, "Autonomy and Socialization," *Mind* 89, No. 356 (October, 1980), pp. 565–576.

31 On the notion of *prima facie* right, *see* footnote 3. When a person's actions violate another's rights it may be necessary to override the *prima facie* rights of the violator for purposes of punishment. Perhaps more aptly, the criminal may be said to forfeit his or her right to freedom of movement when incarcerated for the violation or abuse of the legal rights of another.

32 *See* footnote 18.

33 One clear line of argument for assigning fundamentally unequal rights to persons is to find such a rationale. *See* Wasserstrom, "Rights, Human Rights, and Racial Discrimination" in Lyons, *op. cit.,* pp. 55ff. If we do not deny any of these human rights to the mentally unfit, it may be because (1) we still regard them as persons, if not completely so, and (2) we feel their lives would be significantly impoverished without them. For similar speculations on the rights of such persons, *see* Feinberg, "On the Rights of Animals and Unborn Generations" in Wasserstrom, *op. cit.,* pp. 583ff.

34 *See* Vlastos, *op. cit.,* p. 40. This condition will become important when we consider whether or not one can consent to be treated as a sex object, i.e. consent to unequal moral treatment, *infra* Chapter II, section 3 and Chapter IV.

35 *See* Vlastos, *op. cit.,* p. 52.

36 Whether or not this causal connection exists is taken up in Fred R. Berger, "Pornography, Sex, and Censorship" in Wasserstrom, 2nd. ed., *op. cit.,* pp. 339ff. *Also see* Ann Garry, "Pornography and Respect for Women," in Bishop and Weinzweig, *op. cit.,* pp. 130ff.

37 *See* Garry, *op. cit.,* pp. 133ff.

38 This is one reason why racist attitudes seem to occupy as much of a controversial role as racist practices, whether such attitudes motivate those practices or not. *See* Wasserstrom, "Rights, Human Rights, and Racial Discrimination," in Lyons, *op. cit.,* pp. 55ff.

39 For a similar theme about the sexual relations between men and women, *see* Kathleen Barry, *Female Sexual Slavery* (Englewood Cliffs, New Jersey: Prentice-Hall, 1979); *also see* Michael Korda, *Male Chauvinism! How It Works* (New York: Ballentine Books, 1973).

40 For example, *see* Eames, *op. cit.,* p. 141 and Korda, *op. cit.,* p. 102. *Also see, infra,* Chapter III, section 2.

41 In particular, *see* Sandra Lee Bartky's analysis of sex objectification in "On Psychological Oppression" in Bishop and Weinzweig, *op. cit.,* pp. 36–38. *Also see* my detailed criticisms of her approach, *infra,* Chapter III, section 2.

42 Simone deBeauvoir in *The Second Sex* excerpted from *Philosophy of Women: Classical to Current Concepts,* ed. Mary Briody Mahowald (Indianapolis, Indiana: Hackett Publishing Co., 1978), p. 196.

43 *Ibid.,* p. 191.

44 *See* Catharine A. MacKinnon, "Feminism, Marxism, Method, and the State: An Agenda for Theory"; *Signs: Journal of Women in Culture and Society* 7, No. 3 (Spring, 1982), pp. 530–531: "Socially, femaleness means femininity, which means attractiveness to men, which means sexual attractiveness, which means sexual availability on male terms. . . Gender socialization is the process through which women come to identify themselves as sexual beings, as beings that exist for men." Also p. 538: "Woman through male eyes is sex object, that by which man knows himself at once as man and as subject." *See also, infra* Chapter II, section 2B.

45 *See* Susan Brownmiller, *Against Our Will: Men, Women and Rape* (New York: Simon and Schuster, 1975), Susan Griffin, "Rape: The All-American Crime" and Susan Rae Peterson, "Coercion and Rape: The State as a Male Protection Racket" in Vetterling-Braggin, Elliston, and English, *op. cit. Also see* my discussion of a woman's "rape mentality" *infra* Chapter II, section 4A.

46 The example of two persons in such relations is only the paradigm here. I do not mean to exclude members of group sex from having sexual relations with one another or the woman (or man) who masturbates from having such relations with herself. The limiting factor would seem to be to what extent we can legitimately call the masturbator's attitudes and actions toward herself "relations with" that self. I am not using the expression "sexual *relationship*" for such encounters, since the expression connotes a more purposeful, reciprocal, even physical sexual relation. ("Those two have had a sexual relationshp for ten years.")

47 For a review of the physiology of human and (other) animal sexual behavior, *see* Neil R. Carlson, *The Physiology of Behavior* (Boston, Massachusetts: Allyn and Bacon, 1977), Chapter 11. For some philosophical analyses of the concepts of a sexual interest, sexual arousal, and sexual desire, *see* Roger L. Taylor, "Sexual Experience," *Aristotelian Society (New Series)* 68 (December 11, 1967), Section 1, and Jerome Shaffer, "Sexual Desire," *Journal of Philosophy* 75, No. 4 (April, 1978).

48 For some discussion of such a view, *see* Garry, *op. cit.,* pp. 136ff. For further criticisms of her analysis of sex objectification, *see infra* Chapter III, section 3.

48 Perhaps this is the difference (if there is one) between the portrayals of women in pornography versus so-called "erotic art," the former to be found in "adult" bookstores and underground cinema, the latter in some public libraries and many museums.

chapter 2

Institutionalized Sexual Politics

In the first chapter, we developed a characterization of sex objectification with the dehumanization of the sex object as its central theme. This characterization allowed us to distinguish objectionable from unobjectionable cases of treating persons as objects, and provided us with a source of explanation for the more specific objections the sex object has. We can now investigate some of those objections in more detail to give a characterization of sex objectification in its final form.

The first section of this chapter is devoted to an investigation of any special problems or significance that dehumanization in one's sexual relations might have that it would not have in other personal relations. The second section addresses the complaint that treating women as sex objects is sexist treatment. Included in this section is a characterization of sexism that explains why some sex objectification is considered sexist, as well as an examination of how sex objectification tends to stereotype women on the basis of their sex as the sexual subordinates of men. A brief analysis follows of some of the ways in which the male sexual stereotype may be comparably undesirable. The chapter also examines what it would mean to treat oneself as a sex object, and investigates some of the important asymmetries there are between the way men are treated as sex objects and the way women are treated as sex objects in contemporary society. We will then have examined a sufficient variety of cases to give a characterization of sex objectification in its final form.

1. THE SIGNIFICANCE OF SEX IN SEX OBJECTIFICATION

An important feature of our characterization of sex objectification is that the sex object's ability to attract or excite her objectifier sexually is the vehicle and source of her dehumanization. She is dehumanized through her sexuality, as if it were a feature of her personality that invited her dehumanization. Sex objectification is necessarily dehumanization in the context of one's sexual relations with others. Thus, any analysis of the complaints about sex objectification would be incomplete without some reference to our attitudess about sex and our own sexuality, when such attitudes may make a difference in the way the dehumanization occurs.

A. Sex and Privacy

When the sex object is dehumanized, she typically feels some physical and/or psychological distress and/or some constraints on her freedom of movement and expression. A particular complaint that both the free spirit and assistant manager raise is that they feel their privacy has been invaded by their objectifiers. What could they mean by this accusation? They must feel that some sort of information or knowledge about themselves has been gained by their objectifiers which they would rather have kept to themselves alone, but what sort of information is this? We have assumed that the construction workers were complete strangers to the free spirit, and we can suppose that the assistant manager's complaint has nothing to do with going beyond the information available in an employee dossier.

Recall that the free spirit felt as if her construction workers were looking right through her dress at her naked body, and when the assistant manager guesses at the sexual fantasies of her president, she shudders at the humiliation of it all. But no one's body is actually being exposed to public view. In fact, it is only the unhappy wife whose body is exposed to her objectifier, and she is the one sex object who does not complain about privacy. Her complaint is about an intrusion on her sleep, not a gaining of information that has heretofore been kept private from her objectifier.

The failure of the unhappy wife to see her situation as an invasion of her privacy seems to stem from at least two facts: (1) the setting of her sex objectification is itself a private one, viz. her own bedroom, and (2) her sex objectifier is her sexual intimate, not a stranger to her. When the construction workers or the company president approach their sex objects with sexual overtures, they do so in much more public settings than the bedroom, and they do so as strangers, or at least, as persons on less than intimate terms with the sex object. Even if no one else hears or knows about such overtures, the fact is that one's sexual parts or sexual merits are not typically thought to be appropriately observed by such persons, or discussed with them in such settings.[1] However, this sense of the private is to be distinguished from a discussion or fantasy which those same persons might have about the private dinner table conversation or evening meal the sex object engaged in with her family the previous night. Such activities as eating with one's family at home are activities done in the privacy of the home, but they are also done in public restaurants and recreation spots. Eating, in our culture, is not a private kind of thing for which it is typically inappropriate that persons with whom we are not familiar observe us or discuss our behavior with others.[2]

On the other hand, while the public display of sexually stimulating body parts in strip shows and massage parlors may be a common feature of our culture, it is traditionally considered part of the cultural underground, if not a sign of cultural deterioration. Adam and Eve, upon eating from the Tree of Knowledge, clothe their genitals, not their mouths, arms, or legs. And the typical Victorian married couple were known to have sexual intercourse fully clothed (in "nightclothes") in part, to avoid the embarrassment of visually confronting one's own and the other's genitals in the sex act. In Western culture, one's sexual parts are swathed in a certain mystery and are traditionally associated with a kind of forbidden activity (except under the rubric of a sanctifying marriage) that other parts of the body and the activities associated with them are not (see section 1B). The free spirit would limit the imaginative curiosity the construction workers have about her body because she considers her sexual parts to be private kinds of things, not appropriately observed or discussed (or imagined?) by the public at large. What it would mean to violate one's right to privacy in such instances, then, is for a person to act as if she or he were the appropriate person to discuss or observe one's private parts, when in fact she or he is not. Such a person is curious about or talks about someone's private parts with the same air of propriety as one with whom she or he was on much more intimate terms. Part of the embarrassment that someone like the free spirit may feel comes from a kind of sexual self-consciousness around those with whom she is less than intimate. If she feels especially humiliated, it may be because she finds even a symbolic or imaginative public exposure of her body humiliating in a society which places a censure on such exposure.

Privacy affords a kind of intimacy and spontaneity in one's sexual relations with other persons that is lost, or much more difficult, without it. For many persons, sex in its ideal state is an expression of affection, of trust, and of a willingness to share one's private parts with others on the basis of that trust. Indeed, sex seems to be a way for many to express a level of intimacy that no platonic friendship, however close can match. The physical nakedness of two lovers projects both a physical and emotional vulnerability, which the partner trusts the other will not use against him or her. Such vulnerability simply makes it imprudent to expose oneself to public contact. In fact, this physical openness allows each partner to share in the other's body, to become familiar with that body and to take part in and enhance its bodily pleasures. Affection becomes tied to this ideal, because one's affection for another is conducive to caring about and enhancing another's pleasure and being sensitive to any hesitation or interest the person with that body may have. The suggestion is that privacy in sex affords a kind of trust, familiarity, and affection upon which one's ability to be intimate with one's partner is based. It also has been suggested that since our intimates are by definition the kinds of persons who know things about us that others do not, privacy is necessary for intimacy. Indeed, on this view, privacy is what allows us to separate friends from strangers.[3]

Furthermore, privacy in sex affords a kind of spontaneity that would be lacking if we were constantly aware of a presence or the possibility of a presence of someone else.[4] Recall the paranoia that the free spirit begins to feel when she wonders how many other strange men have given her body the close scrutiny (paralleling X-ray vision) of the construction workers. So too, the assistant manager was notably not "on her guard" when lunching with the company president since she did not, at the time, see his attentions as those of a stranger intent on gaining access to her more private parts. Clearly then, given the lack of familiarity, affection, and trust that the free spirit and assistant manager have with or for their objectifiers (the free spirit is even worried about rape), they see their sex objectification as an invasion of a private domain especially reserved for the intimate. Their inhibitions about what to do next or how to act in the future are a direct result of this invasion. Moreover, if they see their sex objectification as a violation of a particularly personal domain, it is because their objectifiers have taken upon themselves the task of directing the course of their sexual affairs when the women believe such a course must be directed in an important way by their own sexual interests as well as those of their partners. Thus, even the unhappy wife may take her sex objectification as a "personal affront," because she has trusted her husband to share in the love-making experience instead of taking it upon himself to determine what both his and her sexual needs are.

Such considerations may help explain why it is we may want privacy in our sexual relationships, but we can also speculate here as to the reasons why we place a cultural taboo or censure on public sexual exposure. The reasons may be purely anthropological: sex leaves one physically vulnerable to the elements and emotionally preoccupied in a way that, without the privacy and protection of the cave, would make one's survival or successful procreation less likely. Sociobiologists would also argue that the availability of one's sexual parts to public observation and intercourse would severely weaken one's own gene pool, and that since one's genes are "selfish" and willing to combine only with the most desirable genes of other persons, one is simply not directed by one's genes to display oneself publicly to all comers.[5] Psychoanalysts suggest that the taboo on the public exposure of our sexual parts is a necessary sublimation of our id impulses, without which no civilization could progress.[6] Western theology also has a place in such speculations; according to Christian teachings, one ought to be ashamed of the failure to control one's sexual urges, since it is only a reminder of our original fall from grace (where prior to the eating of forbidden fruit, Adam and Eve could control such urges).[7] Sex within the confines of a sanctifying marriage gives a kind of private outlet for such urges. But if one finds oneself drawn to sex outside the confines of this private sphere, one is liable to public exposure and humiliation (remember Hester Prynne's display of her "A" or the puritan stocks). The privacy of the marriage bed itself, depending on which biblical interpretation one uses, might vary from an establishment of the husband's private property rights over his wife to the necessity for intimacy and "spiritual union."[8] In any case, the suggestion is that there are probably good reasons for our Western cultural taboos on sexual exposure, as opposed to the exposure of other parts of our bodies (at least, such taboos do not seem to be just an arbitrary feature of our culture). But whatever reasons we accept, together with the fact that we have our own current and practical reasons for maintaining privacy in our sexual relations, any failure to accord persons privacy in those relations seems to carry with it a special significance that it does not have in other personal relations.

B. Sex as a Defilement of Women

Women may feel humiliated by their sex objectification, then, not merely because no matter what specific rights are involved, they are being demoted from status of moral equal to moral subordinate; they can also feel humiliated by the fact that their sexual parts are being symbolically exposed for public scrutiny in a culture that places a premium on sexual privacy and a censure on public sexual exposure. Yet women have still another reason for finding their sex objectification humiliating, which would not count as a reason if they were dehumanized in other areas of their personal relations. Indeed, it is a kind of humiliation concerning sex that only the women in this culture, and not the men, actually experience. My suggestion is that sex objectification would not be as objectionable for women if there were not two traditional assumptions made about sex generally: (1) that (at least some) sex is dirty, sinful, or evil; and (2) that, because of the distinction made in (1), women fall into two classes, good and bad, virgin and whore, women on pedestals and women in gutters.[9] Moreover, according to one extreme of this tradition, only "bad" women seek, desire, or enjoy sex, while "good" women merely "tolerate" the sexual advances of their husbands and shun completely such advances by those with whom they are on less socially intimate terms. Even if the sex object herself does not subscribe to this general tradition, she knows that her objectifier or witnesses to her sex objectification very possibly do. It may simply be enough to know that the culture to some degree does, even if her objectifier does not. Such a tradition suggests that women are lower on the moral as well as the social register if they can be associated with sex or certain kinds of sex. Women high on the register are morally virtuous women and socially upstanding members of their community. Sex, in this tradition, is the sort of thing which can place women at the bottom of such a register, "in the dirt." Such a tradition has its roots in the Western Christian values of female chastity and obedience to her patriarch. Sex outside of marriage or without patriarchal consent was a defilement of her body and resulted in the lowering of her social and moral status from that of potential wife to mere prostitute or social outcast. In some instances, she was stoned to death by the members of her community.[10] Thus when a woman becomes a sex object for a man, she may feel dirtied or demeaned by him as one associated with a defiling kind of sexuality, in addition to seeing her own sexual interests subordinated to the objectifier's own as per her "object" status. When the sex objectification is public and performed by someone with whom the sex object is less than intimate, all the negative connotations of the prostitute — mercenary, unclean, valuable solely in virtue of her sexual instrumentality for others — arise.

The interesting fact about such images is that they do not typically occur in the minds of men who are the subjects of sex objectification by women. Recall the man who wonders why women do not like being treated as sex objects (read: objects of sexual desire), because he wishes someone would treat him that way. There is no uninitiated (?)/gigolo distinction for men; sex does not make men "dirty." In fact, heterosexual sex is thought by many to turn a mere boy into a respectable, fully developed man. Such sexual asymmetry is simply an outgrowth of our cultural double standard for men and women. In the patriarchal culture of contemporary Western society, the role of men is to rule and provide, while that of women is to obey and support the rulers and providers. In such a society, women are considered the subordinates of men, not their moral equals.[11] The sexual sphere is no exception. Sex does not turn women into the moral equals of men. The brand of respect they do receive is that for a special breed of what is considered to be a fundamentally inferior person who is "pure, delicate, and fragile . . . [with] more refined sensibilities" than men.[12] One is here reminded of the Sunday school teacher, one's mother, and usually, but not always, the wife. Furthermore, in so far as even the ones highest on the pedestal are usually socially, economically, or politically dependent upon and subordinated to the men with whom they live, such "respect" is only a superficial sort of aesthetic appreciation for what is regarded as a type of fundamentally inferior or second-class person. The dehumanization of women in their sexual relations with men is but a reflection of their subordination in other areas of their lives.[13] But the subordination in this sphere has a particularly numbing effect on women, because of the added humiliation which comes with the realization that a *sex* object is often considered to be a low-grade, even dirty, definitely second-class woman of an already inferior type. An examination of the oppressive nature of both the male and female stereotypes involved in sexual relations follows below in section 2.

C. Sex, Self-Respect, and Self-Development

The sort of privacy invasion as well as the added humiliation of seeing themselves as demeaned by sex that often occurs when women are treated as sex objects makes many lose a modicum of self-respect that they do not lose in other areas of their lives. That is, after enough of the sort of treatment described above, women often begin to believe what their sex objectifiers typically believe, *viz.* that their own desires about how and by whom their bodies shall be treated are of only secondary importance when compared to those of the men with whom they come in contact. The peer pressure women feel from men to serve their sexual needs first and foremost is often great, especially in a culture in which the socio-economic power is in the hands of men and can be used as a means of gaining sexual favors. Indeed, such power may simply be assumed to transfer from the political to the sexual sphere, as the appropriate and consistent reflection of the power relations in society as a whole. Sex objectification, then, becomes an expression of the pervasiveness of male dominance and male power under which women live; as object/thing defined in terms of her sexual attractiveness to men by men (the autonomous "subjects" or objectifiers), her own sexuality becomes a source for her continued oppression.[14] It is not difficult to understand why women acquiesce to the sexual pressures of men (only to reinforce the pressure on those who hold out), if they see themselves as politically powerless, and when they see everything from personal attention to financial security to be gained by their own sex objectification. Thus, they not only come to regard their own sexual interests as of secondary importance to those of men, but that this is the appropriate attitude for women to take. As a result, it has been thought to be necessary to raise men's and women's consciousness from the depths of this mentality to see women's moral status for what it truly is.[15]

Moreover, the loss of this sort of self-respect may be especially significant because, according to some, sexual relations are an important vehicle for self-development.[16] Sex provides a means of expressing one's feelings, of "mastering one kind of body language."[17] Successful sexual relations often demand careful consideration of each partner's sexual needs and interests; one learns to share one's experiences with another and learns about one's own sexual needs through another. One who feels or is made to feel that one's sexual interests are not worthy of pursuit for their own sake would never take advantage of the vehicle for self-development and self-knowledge that sexual relations offers. While one's self-development may be enhanced in other areas besides the sexual, one's loss of self-respect in sex is the loss of an important source for such development. Moreover, it can lead one to infer that, if one's sexual interests are of secondary importance, perhaps one's other interests have the same status as well.

An interesting bit of speculation remains: sociobiology and other sexual determinants aside, suppose we were to get rid of the traditional views about sex and sexuality listed above. That is, suppose the dominant culture valued communal living and communal sexual experiences, as opposed to the more private, secluded ones we do now. And suppose we had no history of women dirtied or demeaned by their sexual experiences. Furthermore, suppose we lived in an androgynous society in which there were no social role expectations which attached to one sex, in virtue of that sex, and not the other.[18] What would sex objectification look like in such a world? Would it even exist?

First, one might argue that the kind of sharing of goals that a communal lifestyle seems to demand would considerably weaken the tendency to subordinate one's sex partner inappropriately. As we will argue in Chapter IV, if we are to rid the sexual sphere of any such subordination, we must rid the social, economic, and political spheres of any kinds of inappropriate power play that would foster similar treatment at the sexual level. However, the simple move from private to public sex is not equivalent to such a radical shift. Furthermore, in an androgynous society, although women would not be expected to be the proper sexual subordinates of men solely in virtue of being women, this does not mean that no person would be treated in this way. So suppose that, in the world I have described, there are at least some isolated instances of sex objectification. I would then argue that for women particularly, the psychological damage that sex objectification could do would noticeably diminish. They might still be harmed, angered, or intimated in sex, but the humiliation or embarrassment that would accompany the usual violation of privacy in such instances would be absent or less conspicuous in a culture that placed little or no value on privacy in sex. Even one's inclinations toward playing some sort of decisive role in the determination of one's sex life might be less strong in a society that valued communal over individual sexual pursuits. Thus the "personal affront" the sex object in our own culture feels when dehumanized might be considerably less an affront, or no affront at all.

Furthermore, the added humiliation for women that comes from associating sex with sin would also be absent. One might lose one's self-respect in sex through the blatant disregard that one's partner had for one's sexual interests, but not through the kind of humiliation described above. In addition, women as a group would not be continually subjected to treatment that was picked out by the prevailing cultural ideology as appropriate treatment for them. Thus, a sense of being "victimized" in virtue of one's sex by the prevailing ideology would disappear.

What these observations suggest is that if we want to decrease or eradicate the occurrence of, and damage done by, sex objectification, then we should set about changing the specific sexual attitudes that seem to add insult to the injury of being dehumanized. An examination of the sorts of sexual attitudes that might approach an ideal of moral equality in sex is included in Chapter IV. Sex objectification will continue to exist in any society where at least some individuals, regardless of their sex, and regardless of the absence of the kind of sexual attitudes described above, are thought to be the proper moral subordinates of their sex partners when they are in fact their moral equals.

The construction workers imagined the free spirit as appropriately serving their sexual needs, but not their building or monetary needs. The unhappy wife's husband cannot appreciate her desire for reciprocity in sexual intercourse, although he may welcome the free exchange of ideas in verbal intercourse. And the president offers the assistant manager a promotion in exchange for sex, as opposed to demanding a financial kickback or free use of her new Ferrari. The claim has been that the addition of the sexual component gives the dehumanization in our three examples a special significance and creates special problems that dehumanization in other spheres do not have. Such significance is due to the nature and significance of sex in our own lives.

Our sexual parts are traditionally conceived of as private parts in a way other parts of our bodies are not. Thus, to presume that one was the appropriate observer or documenter of such parts when one was not might be a greater violation of privacy than the same presumption about one's arms or ears. Our sexual parts are at least as vulnerable to careless handling as any other parts of our bodies, and more so than many. And the privacy in our sex lives affords a kind of trust, familiarity, and affection to be built up for one's partner, upon which a valued kind of intimacy in sex is based. So too, we value spontaneity in sex as perhaps a necessary feature for the maximum enjoyment of it, and without knowing one can have sexual relations in private, such spontaneity diminishes.

Furthermore, sex provides a unique vehicle for demeaning women as less morally virtuous or socially esteemed when connected to certain kinds of sexual activity. And if their general humiliation by others continues, women can lose a kind of self-respect for their own sexual needs which, among other things, diminishes their capacity to use sex as a vehicle for their own self-development. The point is that the act of dehumanization, which can violate one's rights to privacy, harm, and exploitation, one's rights to self-respect and self-determination, and tends to reject one's ideals of intimacy, is especially objectionable in relations such as sexual relations, which tend to place some sort of premium on the exercise and pursuit of those very rights and ideals. And because sex and sexual relations seem to have a special kind of significance in our lives, not the least of which is the ability to communicate a level of intimacy that other relations cannot, dehumanization in one's sexual relations will have a significance in our lives that it will not have in other areas.

Given the significance of sex we have mentioned above, one might be surprised that the sex objectification of women by men is so prevalent in our society. Perhaps we simply make more of the phenomenon because of the especially objectionable nature of dehumanization in sexual relations. However, it is more likely that our sex lives are typically such a significant part of our daily lives that the prevalent social and political oppression of women by men cannot help but reach into the sexual sphere of our lives as it does in other spheres.[19]

2. SEX OBJECTIFICATION AS AN INSTANCE OF SEXISM

Let us call an attitude or practice "sexist" when entertaining the attitude or engaging in the practice involves arbitrarily or unjustifiably assigning a character trait or social status to members of one sex in virtue of their sex. A sexist is someone who entertains sexist attitudes, and, in light of those attitudes, engages in sexist practices. Thus, a sexist is a person who labels a man or a woman, because one is a man or a woman, as a certain kind of person, without sufficient evidence for assigning the label, or in the face of verifiable evidence to the contrary.[20] On this reading, a sexist can be a male or female making references about some other male or female, based upon a view about the typical male or the typical female. Sexism is characteristically marked off as a kind of prejudice against women, and since I am interested in this section in the way the sex objectification of women involves sexist treatment against them, the reader may regard sexism in this restricted sort of way. However, when we discuss the various asymmetries there are between the way men treat women as sex objects and the way women treat men as sex objects in section 4 I shall compare the occurrence of any sexist attitudes toward women and toward men, respectively, in each. For such comparison, the term "sexism" or "sexist" shall be used to refer either to prejudice against men *qua* men or to prejudice against women *qua* women. Where the context is unclear, reference will be made to "sexism against men" or "sexism against women." However, this is not to suggest that the two types of sexism are in any way comparable in their pervasiveness or detriment to those who are the objects of the prejudice. Furthermore, I do not mean to overlook the fact that the sexism against women in contemporary society is a feature of a set of larger social institutions and a part of a cultural ideology in which the power and advantage in that society are placed in the hands of men.[21] Recall in the previous section how the sex objectification of women seemed reflective of their subordination or lack of power or prestige in other areas of their lives. The aim is to characterize sexism in terms of assigning sex stereotypes to persons; these stereotypes in their turn generate role expectations for both sexes in their sexual relations, expectations that are fostered and reinforced by a cultural ideology and set of social institutions in which women are the moral subordinates (as opposed to the moral equals) of men. In this way, sex objectification and the sexism typically involved with it can be placed squarely within the patriarchal social milieu in which they occur. Indeed, any consent to one's own sex objectification must be evaluated in terms of its ability to reinforce and perpetuate the existing social inequities between the sexes (see Chapter II, sections 3B and 3C, and Chapter IV).

With these considerations in mind, let us give some examples of sexism and sexists. A sexist is someone who arbitrarily holds the conviction that women cannot take the pressures of corporate life and so refuses to hire any woman for anything other than secretarial or clerical work. A sexist is someone who believes that men ought to pay for their dates' expenses, for the sole reason that men are supposed to "provide" or "take care of things" or "take charge" in their relations with women, even when those women are willing and able to pay for themselves. A sexist is someone who believes that women generally have no aptitude for math, because none of his sisters do, and he refuses to change his views even when he discovers that a woman has taken the high school mathematics prize. (Such occurrences represent "flukes" or are regarded as instances of cheating, trading sex for the prize, or acting too much "like the man.") The sexist derives his beliefs about certain members of one sex from a further belief about the typical or standard member of that sex; moreover, that belief is one which has been made without sufficient or verifiable evidence and which is typically unfavorable or disadvantageous (although it need not be) to those who fall under the standardization.

Given this description of sexism, the three examples of sex objectification described in Chapter I can be considered variations on the following sexist theme: women are, or ought to be, primarily if not solely, sexual servants to male desire. Moreover, it can be argued that such a theme prevails in any sexist case of sex objectification. The variations on this theme are many. The three that occur in our paradigm cases are that (1) women want to be the sexual servants to male desire or cannot help being such servants (the free spirit); (2) it is a woman's duty to be such a servant (the unhappy wife); or (3) women can profit by being such servants (the assistant manager). The female sex object is an object and not also a moral equal in so far as she is used by men for their sexual enjoyment in the (false) belief that such use or appropriation derives from the right and proper place of women as sexual subordinates to men. The construction workers assume that the free spirit has dressed herself primarily with an eye toward pleasing men and wonder why it is that women who do so act so surprised when they are approached by strangers. Moreover, even when we stipulate that the husband respects his wife as a fellow member of the Bar, her primary role as his sex partner is considered by him to be a subordinate one, one which considers his sexual needs as of primary importance over hers and one that he believes all women in their role as wives of men should live up to. In addition, even if we assume the company president recognizes and even respects, in some sense, the assistant manager's organizational abilities, his belief that sex is how women "get ahead in business" derives from a general belief in a patriarchal social system in which women (must) do what men want to succeed (within certain limits) in that system.

A. Sexism and Male Chauvinism

For a man to think that women are or should be the sexual subordinates of men is a much narrower claim than the conviction that the world should be dominated by men, or that the world of moral equals consists of nothing but men. The latter sort of claim about the status of men as some sort of master class of persons is what I take to be the underlying assumption of the male chauvinist. Thus, feminists decry the exclusive use of the term "man" to refer to the human race as an instance of male chauvinism, and see an all-male Federal Supreme Court as symbolic of a male chauvinist attitude toward women on the judiciary. Male chauvinism thus entails sexism against women in so far as women are part of the world that the male chauvinist classifies as inferior, defective, or simply less deserving of respect as persons.

However, sexism against women need not entail male chauvinism, although it often does (and is thus confused with it), because a sexist, in order to be a sexist, need not label women as properly male-dominated in all aspects of their lives, or as inferior to men at all. So, for example, the construction workers, husband, and company president may feel that women are the proper sexual subordinates of men.

But the husband certainly need not think of women as the subordinates of men in the legal profession; indeed, he clearly treats his wife as a moral equal in such a context. And the company president may see nothing wrong with an intelligent woman on the Supreme Court, even though he may wonder, in sexist fashion, what beds she climbed into to get there. Even the sexist who thinks women make lousy mathematicians may think most men do too, but at least he has verifiable and sufficient evidence for the latter claim. Therefore, the proposition "Person P is a sexist" does not entail the proposition "P is a male chauvinist" for every case of sexism. Thus, while someone who treats a woman as a sex object may be motivated by male chauvinism, such motivations do not follow from the fact that the treatment may be sexist. And if one's sex objectification is male chauvinistic, then one's sex objectification is necessarily sexist.[22]

Before we go on to discuss the sorts of stereotypes involved in sexist cases of sex objectification, it should be pointed out that not all cases of the sex objectification of women are instances of sexism against women. A man might regard some woman, or small group of women, as his proper sexual subordinates, but fail to think of the typical or standard woman in that way. Or a man might act toward some woman, or small group of woman as if they were his sexual subordinates, but fail to act toward many or even most other women that way. For an attitude or practice to be sexist, it is necessary to think or act in ways that create and enforce a prejudicial view about members of one sex as opposed to members of another sex by reference to the so-called "typical" or standard member of that sex. Without reference to such a standard, no sex objectification can correctly be considered sexist.

However, this is not to suggest that a sexist cannot have or pick out what he considers to be his own personal sex object. Although the unhappy wife thinks she could be any sexy body, her husband probably wants to have sex with *her* and dominate *her,* not just anyone. And the company president may be able to find other women from which to extract sexual favors, but he may also be especially attracted to this particular assistant manager. Such considerations simply suggest that even though the objectifier may be a sexist of some description, he need not regard the sex object as some de-individualized sexy body which can be used, like any sexy body, to satisfy a sexual need.[23] In short, whether or not the sex objectification is sexist or the object uniquely sexy to the objectifier, the necessary ingredient to the sex objectification itself is the treatment of the sex object as less than a moral equal by her objectifier.

B. Sex Discrimination and Sex Stereotypes

Given the preliminary characterization of sexism above, we can conclude that sexism is an instance of unjust or unwarranted sex discrimination. In those cases of sex objectification that we want to call sexist, the objectification is unjustly discriminatory in so far as it assigns a role to women in their sexual relations with men, based solely on the fact that they are women, in a manner that is neither biologically, socially, nor psychologically justified, but is based on bias or prejudice against them as women.[24] Furthermore, the nature of such discrimination implies the assignment of a sex stereotype to women. Let us call the assignment of any stereotype an assignment of probability or likelihood: if X has feature Y, then X very probably also has feature Z. If X is fat, X is very likely lazy and low in self-esteem; If X is black, X is very likely a good dancer with "good rhythm". Such assignments pick out an often, but not always unfavorable characteristic or nucleus of characteristics which is considered to be essential to identifying the case stereotyped. And this assignment is a conventional one, one that members of any one community who assign the stereotype commonly recognize. However, stereotypes are notoriously applied to more cases than the evidence warrants. So, while some fat people may be low in self-esteem, such data is insufficient for assigning the likelihood or probability of low self-esteem to any fat person one may meet. Thus, a stereotype is an induction based on insufficient evidence, although it is an induction most often based on some evidence or other. As a result, some persons fit the stereotype, either because they constitute the evidence from which the stereotype is drawn or they fulfill (after the fact) the role expectations generated by the stereotype that persons attach to them. So, for example, because some college women pledge for sororities, organize dinners, and root for the home team at all college games, persons have often taken such characteristics of college women to be the stereotype of all college women (witness the epithet "Suzy Sorority"). And in fact, some college women may match the stereotype in response to those role expectations. In such a case, stereotypes literally become the self-fulfilling prophesies of those who formulate them in the first instance.

Sexism against women is an example of assigning *sex* stereotypes to women insofar as the fact that one is a woman is used as the basis for assigning the probability of having a (typically unfavorable) characteristic or social status, even if this does not square with the facts. In so far as sex discrimination implies making such probabilistic assumptions about the members of one sex as opposed to another, it implies the stereotyping of women on the basis of their sex. We introduce this kind of stereotyping in order to argue further that the sex stereotypes inherent in sexism against women generate certain role expectations for women (and for men as well, see below, section 2C); in particular, when those stereotypes are also *sexual* stereotypes, *viz.* stereotypes in sex or sexual relations, they generate certain expectations that women will or should behave sexually in a certain way toward men. So, for example, our sex objectifiers' sexual stereotypes of women take various forms: women want to be sexually dominated by men; wives always want or should want to please their husbands before they please themselves; women cannot rise to the top without having sex with the men at the top. These stereotypes in their turn generate the sexist's role expectation of women that they will, or should, properly subordinate themselves, or be subordinated to the sexual whims of men. Women who are treated as sex objects in sexist fashion are *expected* to act in a way that matches or at least is consistent with the sexual stereotype that the sexist attaches to women.

For those women who see such subordination as oppressive, or unjust subordination, such stereotypes will appear unfavorable. (There are women who will not see such subordination as unjust, and there are those who will not agree that being a sex object demeans them at all. (Sections 2D and 3 below examine consenting to one's own sex objectification.) However, the fact that the stereotype is unfavorable in content is quite a different matter from whether or not the stereotype, regardless of its content, is unfairly restrictive, *viz.* generates role expectations for women which either (1) prevent them from pursuing morally permissible options when they wish to do so; or (2) mold their life choices in a way such that they would never even consider certain choices as viable options for them when there is no justifiable reason for the withholding of such options. Specifically, any stereotype and the role expectations that it may generate are in danger of violating the rights to live a self-determined life of those persons who fall under the expectations, if those expectations involve intimidating, manipulating, indoctrinating, or psychologically dominating those persons into fulfilling one's expectations. This is quite different from suggesting that any role expectations must violate one's autonomy.[25] Indeed, it has been suggested by several philosophers that at least some role expectations, specifically those which do not involve the intimidation and the like mentioned above, can be quite consistent with living a self-determined life.[26] Autonomy does not demand that we be free of all role expectations, only that we be free of overly restrictive or imposing ones. Moreover, if these suggestions are correct, if I have autonomously chosen a particular lifestyle that happens to fit a given stereotype, and thereby am an instantiation of that type, it can hardly be said to constrain my life choices in this respect. The role expectations generated by some stereotypes could theoretically increase one's options, as when the college freshman from the "fine, upper-middle class family" is asked to pledge to a variety of fraternities who would never have asked him but for their expectations that "preppies" such as he will make good frat material.

On the other hand, it is not built into the notion of a role expectation that persons be or feel free to think or act differently than what is expected of them. When women complain that they are expected to identify their self-worth with their sexual attractiveness to men, or to pursue their own sexual needs, desires, and interests only in response to the demands of the men with whom they come in contact, they are complaining not only about the demeaning content of the stereotype which generates those expectations, but also about being confined to such a stereotype by the psychological intimidation and socioeconomic domination of men.[27] In a society that is dominated by men in other areas besides the sexual, pressure from those areas can be brought to bear on women in the sexual sphere to act in certain ways. Thus, as we mentioned in section 1 of this chapter, women may feel they must submit to being sex objects for men in order to gain a kind of social, economic, or political prestige that they would not gain otherwise. Compare how the assistant manager felt intimidated by her boss to have sex or face a career with little option for promotion.[28] But such social prestige as can be exchanged for submitting to one's own sex objectification may be anything from a kind of sexual popularity among one's peers to a real and necessary financial security. Women in the position of our unhappy wife, but who do not have outside careers, often feel they must submit to their husbands' sexual demands or be left without the economic security they have become dependent upon their husbands to provide. In fact, their dependence originates less (if at all) from any actual inability to support themselves adequately than from the belief, reinforced by patriarchal prejudices that prevent women from full and fair employment, that they are unable to support themselves; thus it appears that their inevitable and proper role is to be dependent upon men.

Furthermore, the social status of the women above, such as it is, is a status made available to them only by the approval of those men who define the social power structure. As women continue, however ambivalently, to trade their ability to attract and satisfy men sexually for such limited status, they only raise men's expectations that any woman will be willing to do the same. Thus, it becomes increasingly difficult for any woman to gain and retain social standing within the male-dominated social hierarchy without being the object of sexual intimidation or manipulation by men. Physical appearance may be important to both sexes, but a woman may become convinced that since her society accords her social status only when she can sexually satisfy men, and so only through the men with whom she comes in contact, this is what she ought to value in herself as well.[29] Thus, a woman's sexuality begins to take on a significance for her social worth, and by implication, her self-worth, that it does not for a man. Yet since she is also the constant object of sexual jibes and jokes if, when acting in some professional capacity, she is also attractive ("Must have screwed her way to the top!" "Now that's a woman I wouldn't want my wife to know about!"), her sexuality quickly loses any basis for self-esteem it may have had. And ironically, the extra time she spends preening herself is often chalked up to vanity and is used as evidence that she has better things to do than give her undivided attention to the professional world. (Here the image of the gum-popping secretary filing her nails springs to mind.) Thus, the sexual ideology within which a woman lives reinforces giving special attention to her appearance, only to treat it as a source for her continued domination.[30]

In fact, women reinforce the very sexual ideology that undermines their autonomy by dressing to be the envy of other women, essentially dressing *for women*. They dress for men, certainly, because it is through men that they are typically assigned their value; but they can essentially objectify themselves by urging on each other the very preoccupation with their appearance that is one source of their oppression, a preoccupation unreflectively accepted as normal, natural, and appropriately "feminine." Furthermore, since dressing for women also puts women in competition with other women for the best (male-defined) appearance, they divide their own ranks against the real oppressor, the system of patriarchal values itself.

In addition, the indoctrination of women as the sex objects of men is often subtle and deceptive, so that through carefully selected marketing techniques, for example, women are persuaded to buy the clothes, perfumes, and make-up that tend to reinforce their status as sex objects.[31] Thus, like Suzy Sorority, the expectations of the stereotyper may effectively make the unwitting stereotyped into what she would not be, or would not *want* to be, in the absence of those expectations. For those women who do see their "hidden persuaders" for what they are, they may nevertheless find it practically impossible to change the sexual attitudes of a culture in which male dominance is a central theme. Furthermore, they may find it difficult to convince those women who happily consent to all the sexual attention they get that they are in fact perpetuating a stereotype restrictive to others and fundamentally demeaning to themselves as the moral equals of other persons. Chapter IV presents arguments both for the claim that such consent, given the prevailing sexual ideology described above, is largely unjustified, and that any changes in our sexual attitudes must accompany a change in our socioeconomic and political institutions as well.

In short, women who are expected to be the sexual subordinates of men who complain about those expectations and who recognize them as originating outside of themselves do not only feel their sexual role expectations are unfavorable (because they are demeaning to them as moral equals). Such women also regard these expectations as intimidating, manipulating, or coercing them into leading the kind of lives that they would not otherwise choose to lead. And the very nature of the sexual ideology is such that they are taught to accept uncritically the role of women as the sexual subordinates of men. This indoctrination often keeps them from even questioning whether or not other options might be available to them. Thus, they regard the sexual role expectations engendered by that ideology as in violation of their rights to live self-determined lives free from such incapacitating or debilitating constraints. The stereotype of women as sex objects, then, is a negative or unfavorable stereotype for many women because it categorizes them in a way that is inconsiderate of, if not in violation of, their human rights to well-being and freedom. But it is also unfairly restrictive for those same women in so far as the role expectations generated from it specifically violate their rights to live self-determined lives, lives free, not from all role expectations, but from those expectations that would intimidate, manipulate, or indoctrinate them into living up to those expectations.

In summary, then, the sexism in sex objectification is *prima facie* inappropriate in at least three ways: (1) it discriminates against women on the basis of their sex in a way that is not justified by the facts; (2) it involves the assignment of a stereotype that is unfavorable to many, because the stereotype labels women as moral subordinates and not moral equals; and (3) it involves the assignment of a stereotype that engenders role expectations, which violate the rights of many of those stereotyped to live self-determined lives.[32]

C. Sexual Role Expectations and the Male Stereotype

By distinguishing the unfavorable content of the stereotype from the restrictive nature of it, we can say a few words here about the male sexual stereotype. (More will be said about male sex objects in section 4.) While the female sexual stereotype is one of dependence, submission, and passivity, the male stereotype is one of independence, dominance, and aggression. If anyone is to be treated as the moral equal, indeed moral superior in sex, it is the power-wielding male. In other words, the male sexual stereotype is not one of sex *object*. The content of the male stereotype is not the oppressive one that it is for women. And such a stereotype seems to increase, rather than minimize, a man's ability to live a self-determined life. Indeed, if he is the victim of any sex discrimination in his sexual relations, the bias would seem to be in his favor.

However, it has been argued that not only is such a stereotype restrictive of men's rights to live self-determined lives, but it is in fact an unfavorable stereotype as well. For example, the recent literature on men's liberation suggests that being stereotyped as a relatively insensitive and competitive lover and as one who is interested in his success or performance in bed instead of in the process or experience of the love-making itself is not conducive to affectionate, stable relationships. When men are expected to be relatively callous and carefree in their sexual habits, women do not seek lasting intimacy with them. And, so the argument goes, men are as concerned to maintain such relations as women are. They may be able to exercise their rights in sex, but they are also stereotyped as the sorts of persons who are willing to disregard those of their sex partner in order to exercise their own. Thus, their sex lives are often short-lived, lacking in intimacy or affection, and so very unsatisfactory, because the women whom they meet often expect so little in the way of affection from them. In fact, because such stereotypes are part of the sexual ideology under which boys grow to be men, men readily adopt the stereotype without realizing its detrimental effects on the free expression of their emotions and on their ability to be vulnerable in sex, a vulnerability that would allow them to open themselves to the trust and affection of their partners.[33]

Furthermore, the expectation of sexual mastery and a kind of invulnerability generated by the male stereotype places increasing sexual pressure on men to perform and perform well. While women must lie back and "take it," men are concomitantly expected to be able to "dish it out." Many men have thought such pressures on performance ruin any spontaneity or enjoyment in their sex lives.[34]

However, such pressures on sexual performance are as much a product of a man's own internalized role expectations in sex as they are a product of women's expectations of them. Indeed, many women would like men to think less about performance and more about enjoying the love-making process (recall the unhappy wife), although, given their stereotypes of the average male, they often do not expect their lovers to give that process much weight. And men typically are not intimidated or manipulated by their sex partners into performing on time and on demand. Thus, such pressures should not be equated with the kinds of sexual intimidation and manipulation many women find in their relations with men, which we discussed in section 2B. On the other hand, just as women are often taught to adopt uncritically their role as the submissive partner in sex, so too, many men are indoctrinated to their role as the aggressive partner without thinking to act otherwise. Thus, men readily adopt their sexual stereotype without even realizing they might be more open, more vulnerable, more affectionate in sex, or that this might be socially acceptable, if relatively non-conformist, behavior. Such indoctrination is in violation of men's rights to live autonomous lives in the same way it is for women, since it molds men's choices of their sexual alternatives without their knowledge and without clear justification. Thus like women, men in this position are not free to choose other lifestyles which they might have chosen in the absence of such indoctrination.

Moreover, just as women who subscribe to the prevailing female sexual ideology can bring various sorts of pressure to bear on other, perhaps less willing women to conform to that ideology, men who subscribe to the male ideology can place reasonably compelling social pressures on other men to maintain and exercise their power positions within the socioeconomic or political hierarchy; the concern seems to be that if enough men allow themselves to be vulnerable or dependent or cooperative, the whole patriarchal structure will collapse. And while many men do not enjoy the competitive pressures of being on the top, they find such pressures less distasteful than the lack of power or authority of those at the bottom. Thus, the stereotype is also one of fear at any loss of control, a fear of being intimidated if one is not the intimidator.[35] For those men who do not wish to adopt the role of the dominating, competitive male in or out of sex, the social pressures to continue to play the role set by the stereotype exerted by other men who value their dominant positions may be very real. Such pressures might constitute anything from social snubs to professional blacklisting ("Don't refer any of your ITT clients to Joe's office; he lets all the women in the firm handle the corporate work. I wish he'd knock it off. Now some of the women in my firm are starting to complain that they don't handle enough 'big' cases. Why can't he run his firm like the rest of us?") In short, any pressures that take the form of indoctrinating, intimidating, or even threatening men to accept the masculine ideal are in violation of the right to live a self-determined life of any man so pressured. That is, the expectations that accompany such social pressures can be thought of as restrictive, not simply because they are generated from stereotypes, but because they are generated in a way that would indoctrinate, intimidate, or otherwise pressure freer-thinking men into accepting the role set by the stereotype. The point is that women should not feel that they are the only victims of the prevailing sexual ideology, nor that they cannot perpetuate that very ideology by expecting men to do the very things that neither party really wants. To the extent that both men and women are aware of the power of this ideology and are willing to question its legitimacy, they can begin to structure their sexual relations around that which each individual desires in those relations.

D. Consenting to One's Sex Objectification by Others

Because we have devoted so much time to the claims of those who complain about sex objectification, an explanation is now in order as to why anyone might consent to her (or his) own sex objectification by others, essentially treating oneself as a sex object *for others* (see section 3 below). This section is important for several reasons: (1) it can help us understand the nature of the controversy between those who enjoy being treated as sex objects and those who do not; in particular, it can help us clarify some of the reasons why so many men seem to enjoy being the sex objects of women, discussed in detail in section 4 of this chapter; (2) it is a necessary preface to the section on moral responsibility in which the question is raised as to whether or not those who consent to as well as perpetrate the sex objectification of women can be held morally responsible for acting in exactly the way they are taught and expected to act by the dominant culture; and (3) we must know the reasons why someone might consent to her or his sex objectification before we can evaluate whether or not the consent is justified or permissible under the circumstances.

Consider, then, that in the three cases of sex objectification introduced in Chapter I, none of the sex objects freely consented to their sex objectification, nor would they have consented to it, if asked. In light of this fact, sex objectification was characterized as the violation or *prima facie* inappropriate rejection of the sex object's rights to wellbeing and freedom. However, there are clearly cases of what appear to be sex objectification for which there is no complaint. In particular, given the analysis in section 2B above, there are those who find the sexual sex stereotypes which so often attach to sex objectification neither unfavorable nor restrictive of their freedom to live selfdetermined lives. In reference to women's reactions to advertising above, we mentioned the sex object who thrives on the attention she gets from men. She may work hard to produce the sexual image men

desire and find it presumptuous that anyone should ask her, much less
force her, to do otherwise. There is the barroom stripper who would
seem to make a career out of allowing men to treat her solely as their
sexual toy, tool, prop, or pet; and others act as *Playboy* bunnies as a
chosen sideline, hobby, or for their own excitement. If sex objectification is the *prima facie* inappropriate denial of the sex object's rights to
well-being and freedom, then why would anyone consent to it?

One reason would be that the persons above do not consider themselves the objects of dehumanizing treatment at all. The woman looking for an ego-boost might say that no one is violating any of her
rights, for this is what she wants out of life. For her, peer approval of
the way she is coiffed and dressed makes her feel good about herself in
a way that no other sort of approval can. Unlike the paradigms introduced in Chapter I, she would argue that in this context the way other
people conceive of her is the way she conceives of herself. So too, the
barroom stripper might argue that she is exercising her right to live a
self-determined life by doing what she likes with her body; and no one
is going to diminish her self-image or self-respect, when it is, by
choice, intimately tied to her sexuality.[36] She knows the bouncers are
present to keep her from bodily harm, and she is getting well-paid for
her services. Also, toward the end of section 4 it is argued that the reason why so many men seem to enjoy their own apparent sex objectification by women is that they seldom regard it as dehumanizing at all.
Such comments suggest that if persons can show that they are being
recognized as persons with human rights to well-being and freedom
and that they are treated in ways that do not violate those rights, then
they are not being dehumanized as persons, and so, according to my
characterization, are not being treated as sex objects.

A second reason why persons might consent to their own sex objectification is that while they may realize that they are not acknowledged as the bearers of human rights to well-being and freedom, and
while some of those rights may be violated by others, they would argue that there are other considerations that weigh against the pursuit
of those rights. So, for example, the woman who caters solely to the
sexual attentions of men may acknowledge that she portrays herself as
the sexual subordinate of those men but she likes the free meals, con-
certs, cocktail parties and other favors she gets in the bargain. "Who
cares about subordination when you're having a good time?" she
might ask. The stripper may not in fact think that her routine is the

best way to maintain her self-respect, with the turns and twists she makes over the waving hands of her audience, but the money is good and her agent has a movie contract waiting. The *Playboy* bunny at her photo session might also justify a certain unappealing lack of intimacy or privacy in her circumstances as a necessary (or at least tolerable) means to rather lucrative ends.

Also, as we have mentioned in the pages preceding, a woman may know what her moral rights are, but consent to her sex objectification by others because she sees no other viable alternative. For example, she may feel unfairly intimidated by some man into acting the part of his sexual subordinate (as in the case of the assistant manager) or feel that sex objectification is the only alternative to an unbearable social ostracism. She asserts she would not be acting this way, except for the special circumstances. She feels in some way constrained to act the way she does. Thus, while she consents to be treated as a sex object, her consent cannot be said to be *freely* given.

Furthermore, it is possible, although not the typical consent case, that a woman may feel she must allow herself to be treated as a sex object by men for moral or primarily other-regarding reasons, not merely self-interested or prudential ones. Perhaps the stripper is actually an undercover agent ready to expose the bar in which she works for the illegal pandering of women backstage. Or perhaps the bunny decides the only or most expedient way to give her aging mother proper nursing care is to earn some extra money doing *Playboy* centerfolds. In such cases, their consent to allowing others to dehumanize them would be justified by citing the special circumstances of their own case; they admit that they would not act in such a way but for the balance of good for all concerned which they believe will come of what they do. The point is that the ability of all the women of this second consent category to stimulate or attract men sexually is being used as the vehicle for their dehumanization, and they are in fact dehumanized. But in their individual circumstances, these women simply do not wish to exercise certain of their rights to well-being and freedom when failing to exercise them can bring them other, usually self-interested or practically satisfying ends. They might still react the way the free spirit does, or the unhappy wife or the assistant manager, if in similar circumstances. Even those who see nothing wrong with *Playboy* centerfolds may be annoyed by the harassment of the construction workers or company president. The difference lies in the formers' belief that posing for a centerfold is not dehumanizing at all (some might even suggest that it enhances their self-esteem), while the latter believe it is dehumanizing but that special considerations justify waiving their rights against it.

Such cases are to be distinguished from those of women who consent to their own sex objectification because they do not know that they have claims to certain rights to well-being and freedom or do not understand what those claims are. Such a woman might feel resigned to men treating her as a sex object, because she believes that she is the proper sexual subordinate to them. She does not permit it because she regards it as the means to some worthwhile end. She permits it, because she assumes (wrongly) that she does not have the same rights to well-being and freedom that men do. Moreover, she is one who, unlike the others, might expect something like what happened to the free spirit or assistant manager to happen to her, and feels unhappy, although resigned to accept it as her lot in life. Such a woman typically stops allowing any such dehumanization or at least feels righteously indignant about it, once she is informed of what her true rights are.

On the other hand, there are also those women who may misunderstand what their rights are, but who are happy with the position they have. Such a case is described in the discussion of treating oneself as a sex object for others toward the end of section 3 below. This is the case of the woman who does not think other women are right when they say that they deserve the same rights to well-being and freedom that men do. She thinks that women have different needs and different roles to fulfill in life than men. Why should they fail to serve the sexual (and other) needs of those men, or their husbands at least, who provide them with a home, security, and sex? Moral equality simply sounds like rocking the boat unnecessarily. If such a woman is hooted at from a streetcorner, she may be flustered at the approaches of a stranger, and disgusted by his rudeness. But upon reflection, she is perhaps more likely to think that all he needs is a "good woman," or that his wife is not giving him enough love. And she certainly would not think that the way she acts at home would have anything but beneficial effects for society at large. She supports her husband in all he does; thus he succeeds at what he does. We shall examine the extent to which the attitudes and practices of such a woman may actually have detrimental effects on the society at large in the pages following, and in Chapter IV.

In sum, there seem to be three main reasons why someone might consent to her (or his) sex objectification by others: (1) one sees nothing inappropriate, even *prima facie* inappropriate about one's treatment; (2) one believes special considerations, typically prudential or self-interested ones, justify the treatment, or (3) one does not value the attitudes or actions that attach to treating persons as moral equals, due to ignorance concerning what rights one does have or due to misunderstanding of what those rights are. All such reasons are consistent with the preliminaary characterization of sex objectification given at the end of Chapter I. Specifically, in light of reason (2), the characterization stipulates that sex objectification be only *prima facie* inappropriate; thus, the characterization can reflect the considered judgments of those who think their sex objectification would be wrong but for the special considerations they cite. The questions that remain to be answered concerning the types of consent detailed above are the following: (a) are those persons who see nothing dehumanizing about the treatment we have been calling sex objectification correct in saying so? (b) are the sex objects who would waive certain of their rights in the name of self-interest morally justified in doing so? and (c) is the woman who freely consents to subordinating herself sexually to a man (or men), not in resignation, but because she believes (other arguments notwithstanding) that this is her proper role, morally justified in doing so?

E. Sex Role Expectations and Moral Responsibility

Given that a pervasive feature of the sexual ideology of contemporary Western society is the sex objectification of women by men, and given that those same women and men grow up accepting the sexual role expectations dictated by that ideology, can we hold women morally responsible for consenting to be treated as sex objects? Similarly, can we hold men morally responsible, much less blameworthy, for treating women as sex objects? We typically do not hold persons morally responsible for their actions, if they are done in ignorance of the facts or under constraint or otherwise not under their conscious control.[37] Therefore, if men and women do not know to act any differently than to accept the *status quo*, and if many women are intimidated or coerced into being sex objects, and men are indoctrinated to perpetuate the sex objectification of women — often without even realizing what they are doing — how can we hold them morally responsible for what they do?

Some of those who would reply that we cannot and should not hold persons accountable for their sexual behavior at all are those who see our culture's sexual ideology as determined by certain antecedent causal conditions that make our adherence to that ideology a matter of necessity and not choice. Thus, for example, some sociobiologists might claim that a phenomenon such as the sex objectification of women has survived in our culture (as it has in some form in all cultures) as the species' solution to successful reproduction and procreation. The passive/aggressive roles of women and men, respectively, survive in the culture, because such roles provide the optimal conditions for both the survival and evolution of the species. Such a phenomenon will die out only when it becomes an evolutionary hindrance to this survival.[38]

Along quite different, but no less deterministic lines, it has been suggested that our present practice of allowing the female to be the primary caretaker of the young instills an overwhelming sense of narcissistic rage in the infant against the woman who first forces upon it the recognition that it is not omnipotent (since she is perceived as the giver and taker of food, warmth, etc.) This rage is then projected onto all women in the infant's adult life, part of which translates into women's sexual (and other) subordination by men. The male adult vents its infantile rage on the female; the female adult identifies with her mother while still feeling that same rage herself. She thus ambivalently accepts her male subordination as reciprocation for an earlier power to which she herself was subject but for which she also yearns. (Thus the claim that women are masochists: they identify with the very figure which their unconscious believes is the proper subject of subordination.)[39] Moral philosophers have taken such brands of determinism to suggest that we cannot hold persons morally responsible for what they do, at least in any sort of ultimate sense, since they cannot rightly be said to be able to choose to do other than they in fact do.[40] Men do not choose to treat women as sex objects any more than they choose their eye color; they do so in response to internal mechanisms set in motion outside any human control, or long before men were in a position to decide whether to adopt those controls or not. The above remarks apply *mutatis mutandis* to women who consent to being treated as sex objects by men.

On the other hand, even those who believe in some form of determinism have suggested that we can talk about moral responsibility by taking into account, not the infinite chain of causal conditions which preceded the act in question, but only those causal conditions that have an immediate bearing on the question of whether or not the agent could have acted otherwise than she or he in fact did. To act "freely" in this sense would mean to act with sufficient knowledge of the facts, with a clear head, and without any compelling physical or other immediate external constraints; if one were to act in ignorance or under duress one could not be said to have acted freely, and so would not be held accountable for one's actions.[41]

If we were to adopt such a view, I think that at least some, but not all, persons who either treat others as sex objects or consent to such treatment can be held morally responsible for what they do. Those women who are literally coerced into subordinating themselves to men are exempt from responsibility under the conditions above. And those women who know their rights but who freely waive them in the name of self-interest are those who can be held responsible for what they do. But what of those who act in ignorance or simply in blind obedience to the sexual ideology under which they live? Is not insufficient knowledge of the facts an absolver of responsibility? Or is the ignorance such that persons can and should know better than to act in ways that are *prima facie* wrong, but who for some reason do not know better?

The problem is that while our sexual ideology may often be adhered to unreflectively or without question, the fact that one does not think to do other than what it dictates is not the same as being in no position to know otherwise. And it is the latter, and not the former, feature of human action that absolves persons of moral responsibility for their actions. While part of the moral responsibility, and so part of the blame for any wrongdoing can be placed on the society at large for indoctrinating its members to adopt a sexual ideology that treats women as less than moral equals, it is persons who make and perpetuate ideologies and not some abstract entity called "society." Thus, while persons may be taught certain role expectations and may even feel some peer pressure to meet those expectations, persons can and should still question the legitimacy of them. This is just the posture of those consciousness-raising groups of the last two decades which, among other things, would expose the unfavorable and restrictive nature of our sexual stereotypes for men and women. Indeed, it could be argued that we have been sufficiently informed by feminists of the unjust subordination of women to men that continuing to perpetuate that subordination by treating women as sex objects is a culpable moral offense. So too, according to this view, parents have a responsibility not only to inform themselves of such feminist concerns, but also not to indoctrinate their children to accept the kinds of sex roles that perpetuate the sex objectification of women.

The difficulty with such arguments lies in assessing the extent to which feminism has made clear to the general public the kind of moral damage done by sex roles and sex stereotypes in general, and sex objectification in particular. Many would counter that feminists themselves are so divided on such basic issues as sex equality[42] that other people can hardly be expected to know where to stand on any feminist issue, much less recognize one when it appears. However, this counter does not absolve persons from unreflectively acting in ways that feminists have openly and actively identified as oppressive to women. Sex objectification is one such issue. Admittedly, both men and women may get double messages from strippers on the one hand and consciousness-raisers on the other, but I think that neither sex can be absolved of all moral responsibility for their sexual behavior solely on the grounds that such behavior constitutes the *status quo*. Furthermore, by being aware of the subtle forms that the prevailing sexual ideology can take, women may be less likely to act in ignorance or with a misunderstanding of their moral rights. And they may be less likely automatically to expect men to shy away from intimacy, and so be less likely to perpetuate a male stereotype that both women and men have found unfavorable. Moreover, those who may have formerly mistaken their sex objectification by men for a simple appreciation of an attractve body may see the demeaning attitudes of their objectifiers for what they are and so act to change those attitudes or avoid such contact in the future. So too, men might sooner or more readily acknowledge the restrictive nature of their sexual stereotype and act to change what many now view as an undesirable situation, and those who sacrifice their moral rights for fame or fortune may at least compare what they must do for those benefits against the men with whom they may compete.

If moral responsibility for an action is a pre-condition for assigning moral praise or blame to the agent who performs that action, then, in spite of the prevailing sexual ideology, we can offer some ways of assessing the blameworthiness of the sex objectifier who, in the absence of special considerations, and with the kind of freedom stipulated earlier in this section, treats a woman as a sex object. And if there are any cases in which a woman freely consents to her own objectification but is unjustified in doing so, similar remarks as to her blameworthiness for her actions may be made (for an analysis of such cases, see Chapter IV). So, for example, the man who intends to treat a woman as a sex object and fails may be judged equally blameworthy as he who succeeds, since his moral worth lies not in the objective rightness or wrongness of his actions, but in the quality of his moral motives or intentions.[43] A man who does not know any better than to treat women as sex objects may be absolved of blame, if we can show that he could not, even upon reflection, be expected to know better (e.g., a stranger to the community), or perhaps if the knowledge of his mistake changes the character of any of his future actions, even if he should have known better. Those who inadvertently treat women as sex objects as consequences of other actions may be blamed if those consequences could have been foreseen. And those persons who want very much to stop treating women as sex objects, but who sometimes lapse from want of peer support, may be the least blameworthy of all, even when the actions of such persons exactly match those of the individual who intends to treat women as sex objects. In short, our evaluations of moral responsibility and blame should be tempered by the real pressures, both psychological and social, that can be brought to bear on those living under a sexual ideology that teaches and expects the subordination of women. However, such an ideology should not be used to absolve persons of their moral responsibility to question that ideology and so refrain from thinking and acting in ways that treat persons as less than moral equals.

3. TREATING ONESELF AS A SEX OBJECT

An interesting case of sex objectification to consider is the case of treating oneself as a sex object. This is to be distinguished from merely believing that one has a sexy body or from wearing tight-fitting clothes to show off one's body to its best advantage. And it is to be distinguished from merely believing that one's self-worth is tied in some central way to the fact that one is sexy. To fit our characterization of sex objectification, the case must be one with a *prima facie* negative normative component: the woman who treats herself as a sex object must treat herself as less than a moral equal. She must not only value herself primarily in terms of her sexuality in some context, she must also use that sexuality as the vehicle for her own dehumanization.

A. Masturbation and Dehumanization

What might the project of treating oneself as a sex object entail? First, recall in our characterization of sex objectification that A values B primarily or solely for B's ability to attract or stimulate A, and that A dehumanizes B in the context of A's sexual relations with B. If A is the same person as B, such that A treats A as a sex object, then A must be described as valuing herself for her ability to stimulate or attract herself sexually; A's dehumanization occurs within some context of A's stimulation of or attraction to herself.

Suppose we define masturbation as sexual stimulation of oneself by oneself, not some other person.[44] Then the woman who masturbates will treat herself as a sex object *only if* she dehumanizes herself in doing so. Interestingly enough, the traditional view of masturbation has been that it is necessarily degrading, or, to use the terminology of this discussion, that it is necessarily dehumanizing. Kant regarded masturbation (indeed all forms of non-heterosexuality) as an unnatural act, degrading to the human species. Such an act was regarded as one which "makes man (sic) unworthy of his humanity. He no longer deserves to be a person."[45] Thomas Aquinas regarded onanism (in which masturbation by a male results in the emission of semen) to be "contrary to nature," and so unworhty of a man who was obliged to follow his natural, God-given path.[46] And Freud was convinced masturbation was "by no means harmless" as it predisposed persons to all sorts of neuroses and psychoses, far from sexual activity which met the demands of "civilized sexual morality."[47] However, the view taken here is that masturbation need not be the sex objectification of oneself, although it can be if the masturbator, in the process of masturbation, treats herself (or himself) as less than the moral equal of other persons.

Suppose, for example, that a woman masturbates in public view because she feels she deserves the humiliation that accompanies it. Or suppose she masturbates only on the command of another, even though she enjoys self-stimulation much more often than that and knows her commander will often withhold his judgment simply to dis-comfort her. Such cases suggest that the masturbator must do some-thing more than masturbate to treat herself as a sex object; she must also somehow think of herself or act toward herself as if she deserved less of the rights to well-being and freedom than persons are typically thought to deserve, and therefore masturbate in a way that dehuman-izes her. Her value to herself may be self-imposed in such cases (al-though she may treat herself as a sex object in light of the traditional view of masturbation or the traditionaal view of women found in her culture); even so, it is a value that reduces her to an expendable object and not one that raises her to moral equality. Those who perceive masturbation to be necessarily sex objectifying mistake the fact of self-stimulation for the value-laden phenomenon of self-dehumanization.

B. Changes in the Characterization of Sex Objectification

We will have passed over an important meaning of "treating oneself as a sex object" if we take only the case of the self-stimulator. There is also the case of the woman who treats herself as a sex object for men or for some other person(s) besides herself. We can call such dehumanization "treating oneself as a sex object for others" to distin-guish it from the dehumanizing self-stimulator described above. (The two cases should not be construed as mutually exclusive. One might be both a dehumanizing self-stimulator and one who regards her sex-ual attraction to men as an acceptable vehicle for their dehumanization of her.) Treating oneself as a sex object for others may be more common, and it is the kind of sex objectification of one-self that is most commonly associated with consenting to being treated as a sex object by others, which was discussed in the previous sec-tion.[48] This kind of case is one in which a woman values herself pri-marily in terms of how well she can attract or sexually satisfy the opposite sex, but succeeds in her attraction only by subordinating some or all of her own sexual needs or preferences to members of that sex. In this way, she treats her sexuality as the vehicle for her dehumanization by her own actions. We shall give a full description of such a project below. If she primps and preens herself in narcissistic fashion, she does so not because, in spite of the men around her, she loves herself best, but because she loves the reactions that men have to the way she looks. In the previous section, we mentioned the importance that a woman can begin to place on her appearance in response to the expectations of her peer group and in the belief, fostered by an internalized sexual ideology, that her only real source of self-esteem lies in the way she looks.[49] If she engages in any narcissistic behavior in virtue of such internalized expectations, it is not only because she wants other women who also care about that sort of thing to notice how she looks, but also because she wants to attract or please other men. (Indeed, many heterosexual women care about that sort of thing because they must dress well in order to be acknowledged at all by the male hierarchy of power and prestige.) Thus, we must change our characterization to read that A dehumanizes B in some context C of A's sexual relations with B *or some other person D,* and that A values B in C primarily for her ability to attract A *or D.*

Also, we have been translating treating a person as less than a moral equal as either (1) conceiving of a person as less than a moral equal or (2) acting toward that person as less than a moral equal, or both. Thus, in a discussion of sex objectifying attitudes to the exclusion of similar practices, and practices to the exclusion of attitudes, we wondered whether persons had a right to be thought of as moral equals; a distinction between dehumanizing attitudes and practices was also drawn when we were interested in the blameworthiness of the person who tries unsuccessfully to refrain from acting toward another as a sex object. This distinction was drawn largely in response to the claim that what women are complaining about when they object to being treated as sex objects is not only a way of acting toward women, but also a way of thinking about them. Thus, if a woman is to treat herself as a sex object, she will either (1) conceive of herself in her sexual relations with herself or other persons as less deserving or not deserving of the rights to well-being and freedom that others enjoy, or (2) waive some or all those rights in her sexual relations, or both. Instead of trying to make some conceptual sense out of violating one's own rights, the analysis above suggests that the sex object waive some or all the rights that, as a human being capable of experiencing and valuing a certain level of well-being and freedom she in fact has.

If we make this conceptual move, two options remain: (a) we can stipulate that such a waiver "rejects in a *prima facie inappropriate* manner one or more of the sex object's rights to well-being and freedom" (this is the second disjunct of the first condition of the characterization of sex objectification); or (b) we can stipulate that such a waiver is itself one of the special considerations that justifies sex objectification given the *"prima facie"* nature of the wrong. Waiving one's rights would then be considered perfectly appropriate conduct as long as one did so voluntarily and in full knowledge of the nature of the waiver. The argument presented in the pages following is that we should not accept any waiver of one's rights to well-being and freedom unless the waiver can be justified on the same kinds of grounds that justify the original exercise of those rights. Since the burden would be on the one waiving the right to show that the waiver is justified, this argument favors stipulation (a) above. The argument proceeds by examining the sorts of reasons one might give for thinking that the waiver of one's rights to well-being and freedom in one's sexual relations, and under the prevailing sexual ideology described earlier, is *prima facie* inappropriate. After examining a variety of responses to such reasoning, the conclusion is that the least problematic alternative is to regard the waiver of one's rights to well-being and freedom in the way specified by stipulation (a). Also, as the discussion will show below, waiving one's rights to well-being and freedom comes to permitting other persons to treat one as less than a moral equal. Thus, by examining the reasons why waiving one's rights might be *prima facie* wrong at this point in the discussion, we can set the stage for asking whether or not any reasons for consenting to one's own sex objectification by others can be conclusively justified.

C. Waiving One's Rights to Well-Being and Freedom

Waiving one's rights to well-being and freedom is equivalent to permitting others to treat one in a way that would be in violation of those rights, if one had not waived them. At the very least, if someone does violate those rights, one has no legitimate right to complain.[50] Thus, acting toward oneself as a sex object by waiving one's rights to well-being and freedom in one's sexual relations in a given context will entail giving others one's tacit approval that they may treat one as less than a moral equal. Acting toward oneself as a sex object is essentially allowing, even facilitating, one's own sexual dehumanization by others, since there are no apparent moral barriers to such treatment by others, given the nature of the waiver. I use the expression *"acting* toward oneself as a sex object" because thinking of oneself as a sex object need not entail waiving one's rights to moral equality in sex. A woman may simply think of herself as the proper sexual subordinate of men without going so far as to allow herself to be subordinated by them. Thus *"treating* oneself as a sex object" which can include either conceptions of or actions toward oneself, need not entail consent for others to do so as well.

We have argued in Chapter I that the failure to treat persons as moral equals involved in sex objectification is *prima facie* wrong, viz. wrong unless it can be shown that compelling considerations justify the failure. However, if treating persons as less than moral equals is *prima facie* wrong, then one argument might be that to permit others to treat persons as less than moral equals is to concur in or create an opportunity for others to do something *prima facie* wrong. And as some philosophers have noted, to concur in or create an opportunity for someone to do something wrong is to share in the wrong.[51] One's permission essentially encourages the wrongdoer to act in a way that is wrong and to encourage wrong behavior is itself wrong.[52]

Furthermore, such permission, if continued, can foster and reinforce a climate of legitimacy for failing to treat other persons as moral equals. Those who do not permit their own sex objectification by others, for example, may become expected to do so when enough persons give their own stamp of approval to the phenomenon as a whole.[53] Given the restrictive nature of such expectations for at least some men and women, which was discussed earlier, treating oneself as a sex object can thus create the kind of climate that is in danger of violating the rights of other persons to lead self-determined lives. In short, one might argue that to treat oneself as a sexual subordinate is freely to accept being treated as one by others. But this acceptance encourages one's own dominaton, humiliation, intimidation and the like which we have suggested is the *prima facie* wrongful treatment of persons. And encouraging someone to do something wrong is itself wrong. Furthermore, one's encouragement of one's own sex objectification by others fosters the expectation in the mind of the objectifier that others will or should acquiesce as well. Thus, waiving one's rights to well-being and freedom in one's sexual relations is wrong, unless considerations can be offered that counterbalance the reasons stated above for the wrong.

There are several objections to this way of arguing: one is that we have no way of knowing whether or not what we do will encourage others to act inappropriately toward those besides ourselves; and even if we do, we can hardly keep from acting simply because some person or other, no matter how removed from our present circumstances, might be adversely affected by what we do.[54] In such a case, the problem, it seems, is one of reconciling the competing rights of those who wish to lead self-determined lives, of which their choice to be sex objects is a part, with those who would choose otherwise. Chapter IV investigates the balance of such competing rights.

On the other hand, a different sort of objection to the analysis above is that the *prima facie* wrong in treating persons as less than moral equals means that doing so is wrong *but for the consent* of the persons so treated. There is nothing wrong with waiving one's rights to well-being and freedom, so the objection runs, when the waiver is a voluntary and informed one. Therefore, one does not encourage any wrongdoing, since the objectifier acknowledges the nullifying nature of the consent; neither does it create any climate of intimidating expectations that others will acquiesce, since the consent is, by hypothesis, free of such intimidation.

There are two sorts of responses one can make to this objection. The first is that it is far from clear that the woman who treats herself as a sex object for herself or for others is always making a choice free from the intimidation of others and the indoctrination of her culture's sexual ideology. In fact, some reason was given for thinking this freedom absent for a wide variety of cases of sex objectification in the discussion of sexual role expectations for women and in the discussion of the traditional view of masturbation. On the other hand, it is notoriously difficult to judge the degree to which any social pressure to think or act a certain way is a real and present restriction on a woman's (or man's) autonomy, and to what degree such pressure is simply a natural concomitant of any widely-accepted role expectation in which one is free to do other than what persons expect, but where one may be considered odd, unwise, or simply non-conformist by others for doing so. In particular, if we are to hold at least some men and women in any way responsible for either treating others as sex objects or willingly (and without grudge) consenting to it themselves, then such persons must be or feel free enough from any external constraints or pressures to choose what to do. If we are to argue that at least some women who waive their rights to moral equality in sex are either not fully informed of what their rights are, or are being forced or intimidated or indoctrinated into the role of moral subordinate in sex, then we must be sure that we are not mistaking what seem like inevitable sexual role expectations of some sort for the kind of expectations that actually violate one's right to live a self-determined life within the confines of one's social network.[55]

The second response is that, even if we could show that the waiver was freely made, such a waiver can be said to violate a fundamental principle of morality, viz. the principle that persons ought to treat both themselves and other persons as moral equals. Such a principle might be regarded as a kind of basic principle of morality, because it suggests that all persons deserve a minimum degree of respect from persons as bearers of certain fundamental human rights to well-being and freedom, rights that cannot legitimately be waived by free and informed consent alone. This principle of respect for persons has, in various guises, historically been used to ground a framework for moral choice and moral conduct.[56]

Suppose we accept the claim that to treat oneself or others as less than the moral equals of others violates a fundamental principle of morality. In fact, the moral equality described in Chapter I would seem to provide us with a kind of fundamental foundation for moral conduct, if any such foundation exists at all, because the basis for such equality lies in the shared human capacity to value a certain level of well-being and freedom that animals or objects are considered not to have. Thus, to claim that consenting to one's own sex objectification violates a fundamental principle of morality is not inconsistent with what has been previously argued for.

Nevertheless, we should be careful not to commit ourselves to the overly strong claim that the rights to well-being and freedom guaranteed by such a fundamental principle as that of moral equality cannot be appropriately waived under any circumstances. Given the variety of rights to well-being and freedom listed under the principle — rights to privacy, freedom of movement, expression, and so on — and the variety of reasons one might have for wishing to waive some of those rights, it seems unwise to place so narrow a restriction on them. However, one might still argue that the kinds of considerations it would take to justify voluntary and informed consent would have to be the same kinds of reasons that are used to justify the rights in the first instance. That is, for one to waive one's rights to well-being and freedom appropriately (and so fail to treat oneself as the moral equal of persons) would mean not only that *without* the waiver one would lead an impoverished or unfulfilling life, but also that the waiver must not interfere with the exercise of the rights to well-being and freedom of others. Thus, it has been suggested by Gregory Vlastos that ". . . an equalitarian concept of justice may admit just inequalities without inconsistency if and only if it provides grounds for equal human rights which are also grounds for unequal rights of other sorts."[57] This way of talking about waiving one's rights to well-being and freedom leaves open the possibility that such a waiver can be justified without also suggesting that just any waiver might count; and in this way we are in a position to demand that reasons be given for the waiver when required and to assess those reasons without dropping them out of hand. Furthermore, this condition on justification can also be applied to the case of those who wish to override the rights to well-being and freedom of others. The conclusion is that if treating persons as less than moral equals is in violation of a fundamental principle of morality, as the analysis of moral equality in Chapter I as well as much of the historical literature suggests, then the waiver of one's rights to well-being and freedom as a moral equal will be justified only under very strict conditions. Voluntary and informed consent alone will not automatically justify the treatment. As Vlastos suggests, only the same kinds of grounds that provide the basis for moral equality should provide the justification, if any, for treating persons as less than moral equals. In Chapter IV, we shall consider whether or not the reasons typically given by those who both conceive of and act toward themselves as sex objects, or those who merely consent to their sex objectification by others, satisfy the conditions above.

D. Examples of Treating Oneself as a Sex Object for Others

Since acting toward oneself as a sex object in a given context constitutes waiving one's rights to well-being and freedom in that context, and since such a waiver is equivalent to permitting one's treatment by others as less than a moral equal, any examples of *treating* oneself as a sex object can be described as follows: one may allow one's sex objectification by others whether one also thinks of oneself as a sex object or not; or one may simply think of oneself as a sex object without actually permitting anyone else to treat one that way. Thus we should add to the examples of the sex objectifying masturbator the possibility that she may act in ways which constitute her own dehumanization (thereby waiving her rights to well-being and freedom) without actually thinking of herself as deserving of less respectful treatment; or she may think of herself as worthy only of humiliation when it comes to her own masturbation, yet never act in ways which promote this nor allow others to do so. Examples of treating oneself as a sex object for others further reveal the diversity of cases. For example, a woman may think of herself as the moral equal of any man, but waive her rights to be treated as a moral equal in her sexual relations with men by mistake or under duress or due to a misunderstanding of the treatment from others she expects to receive. In doing so, she permits her own objectification even though she actually conceives of herself as a moral equal all the while. Or she may have good reasons for waiving her rights, even when she believes she is the moral equal of others. Thus, the undercover agent described in section 2D of this chapter may temporarily submit to a dehumanizing striptease in order to convince her employer she is the stripper she purports to be, even though she believes she is deserving of better treatment. And the *Playboy* bunny who poses nude with an eye for the easy money it will bring may nevertheless conceive of herself as the moral equal of any man, even if she feels she has had to give up a certain amount of privacy or tolerate rude and humiliating conduct by the photographer in order to gain her ends. (Of course, she may not think her position is a dehumanizing one at all, and if she can show that the way she acts does not necessitate waiving any of her rights to well-being and freedom, then she cannot be said to be treating herself as a sex object.)

Such women are to be distinguished from the woman who sees herself, for whatever reason, as less deserving of the kinds of rights to well-being and freedom that men enjoy, and so allows herself to be treated as a sex object by others. She may do so because she has a certain conception of herself, distinct from her conception about women generally; or she may consent to being treated as a sex object by others because she truly believes the proper role of any woman is to be the sexual subordinate of men. In either case, she thinks of herself as a sex object for men (or some man), and she acts in accordance with that conception. On the other hand, perhaps less frequently, a woman may consider her proper station as that of the sexual subordinate of men without deeming to act in a way which matches that conception. Perhaps she is tired of being chastised by her feminist friends for allowing men to treat her as a sex object or is too afraid to allow a man really to dominate her in bed. Nevertheless, she believes that the proper role of at least herself, if not all women, is to be the sexual subordinate of men; therefore, she conceives of herself as properly such a subordinate, even though she does not act in a way that parallels her convictions.

Notice that the woman who treats herself as a sex object in the conviction that all women are the proper sexual subordinates of men is one who treats those women as sex objects herself. That is, she may either conceive of women as less than moral equals in their sexual relations with men, or act toward women as less than moral equals in those relations, or both. She may even unhappily resign women to this role when she wishes it were otherwise. On the other hand, she may expect women to be happy with the role they have been given by men in the same way she is happy. Such a woman may believe that any of her married women friends who do not think that they ought to cater to the sexual desires of their husbands before they cater to their own are in moral error. She may even become secretly angry when her friends express their indignation at being expected to subordinate their sexual wishes to their husbands' or to dress only in the clothes that their husbands find attractive. She considers such women to mistake or misunderstand a sort of rightful moral equality for the true and proper role of women as the sexual subordinates of men. And if she not only thinks about women this way, but is also willing to verbalize her beliefs, she might say that she enjoys performing a role for her husband that he clearly values. He takes pride in his role as initiator and aggressor in the sexual encounter and would enjoy sex much less if she were to question the validity of that role. Furthermore, she would say with pride that she is financially secure and socially accepted by her husband's male peers as a woman who obviously knows how to please a man, although she would assert that she does not trade her subordinate role for such things.[58] She may also claim that she is sexually satisfied. For example, she may like it when he "takes control" in sex and would not think of denying him what he demands. In short, she would assert that she gets satisfaction out of seeing his wants fulfilled. She wonders what sort of benefits moral equality could confer on women that they do not already have. This is just the sort of woman who thinks and acts in a way that might be said to encourage men to treat other women as sex objects or to create a climate of legitimacy for their sex objectification.

In summary, then, treating oneself as a sex object may mean conceiving of oneself as a sex object or acting toward oneself as a sex object, and often means both. Acting toward oneself as a sex object comes to waiving some or all of one's rights to well-being and freedom in one's sexual relations. To do so is to give others the option of treating one as a sex object, whether they take that option or not. Conceiving of oneself as a sex object means thinking of oneself as less deserving or not deserving of the rights to well-being and freedom that men enjoy in their sexual relations. This may or may not motivate one to waive the rights one in fact has, and so treat one's own sexuality, both in word and deed, as the vehicle for one's dehumanization. Notice that all of the above is to be distinguished from the simple event of a woman masturbating or even from the preoccupation some women have with how sexually attractive they can make themselves to men. One must dehumanize oneself in one or more of the ways specified above to treat oneself as a sex object. In other words, even if one feels that the one thing one has to offer the world is a sexy body, one has not yet treated oneself as a sex *object* until that conception entails the belief that what one has to offer to the world makes one less deserving or undeserving of the rights to well-being and freedom that other persons enjoy.

In sum, just as one can treat oneself as a sex object (sexually attractive) for others but not for oneself, one can treat others as sex objects, even though one is not sexually attracted to them. One must simply treat their ability to attract others as a feature which makes them less deserving or not deserving of the rights to well-being and freedom that moral equality guarantees. Moreover, those who wish to justify either treating themselves as sex objects or treating others in the same way must seek to justify such treatment on the same grounds as those upon which one's rights to well-being and freedom are based. Voluntary and informed consent of the sex object does not automatically justify treating her (or him) as less than a moral equal. The next section presents the argument that because men's sexuality is not typically viewed by them or their culture as a feature that can reduce them from moral equal to subordinate, they typically do not regard them-

selves or other men as sex objects; rather, when they regard themselves as sexually attractive, they also typically regard themselves as
confident, masterful, relatively independent moral equals or persons.

4. MALE SEX OBJECTS AND FEMALE SEX OBJECTS: SOME ASYMMETRIES

Our paradigm cases of sex objectification have been those of women
treated as sex objects by men. However, heterosexual women can also
be the victims of sex objectification by homosexual women who find
them sexually attractive, as can heterosexual men be the victims of sex
objectification by homosexual men. Furthermore, men have been
known to be the objects of sex objectification by heterosexual women.
Certainly we can imagine the lesbian or gay male being a distant or
insensitive lover in the manner of the husband of the unhappy wife, or
a woman using her corporate position to extract sexual favors from the
men who work under her just as our company president does. Perhaps
then, one can simply substitute men for women and homosexuals for
heterosexuals in our introductory examples of sex objectification,
leaving the attitudes of the sex objectifiers and the reactions of the sex
objects intact. Clearly, however, there is no simple substitution to be
made. At least some men say they love being treated as sex objects, but
by this, do they mean that they love being treated as less than moral
equals, or rather that they love being sexually desirable persons? And
women typically do not have the attitude that their husbands, much
less all husbands, ought to subordinate their sexual interests to their
wives, and women in business typically do not see sex as the major
means of promotion for men. Furthermore, lesbian women often find
their sex objectification by men not only demeaning to their status as
moral equals, but also an irritating presumption that they are interested in sex with men at all. There are some important asymmetries
between the way a woman is treated and the way a man is treated when
they are regarded as sex objects by persons of either homosexual or
heterosexual orientation. And I shall argue that these asymmetries in
treatment help explain the different reactions of women and men to
their sex objectification.

We can stipulate here that a man's sex objectification by another
person shall be referred to as "male sex objectification" and a woman's

sex objectification "female sex objectification." The case of the homosexual male sex object is described as a phenomenon sometimes more akin to female sex objectification than heterosexual male sex objectification, and while sex objectification between lesbians occurs, it may be a less frequent phenomenon than sex objectification between gay men.

Sex is typically a less effective vehicle for the dehumanization of men in contemporary society than it is for women. Thus, men are much less frequently and successfully treated as sex objects by women as women are by them. And when a man is successfully treated as a sex object, the woman or homosexual male sex objectifier has been able to place her or himself in a position of some sort of power or domination over the object.

A. The Female Rape Mentality

One of the reasons why the complaints of female sex objects have fallen largely on deaf male ears is that many men do not understand why women fail to treat their sex objectification as a compliment. After all, they say, women do not really mind being whistled at; in fact, honest women wish it would happen more often. It was suggested earlier that this misunderstanding had to do with the fact that many men see being a sex object as being an object of sexual desire and not as a sex thing or as a sexual subordinate. Thus, on this reading, anyone who did not like being a sex object simply did not like sex.

The interesting fact about this misunderstanding is that it occurs because being a sex object actually means something for many men that it does not for many women. Otherwise, why would it be so difficult for a man to understand the complaint that women do not like being treated as sex objects? Of course, some men may enjoy being sexually dominated by women, and so understand the meaning of the expression "sex objectification" but fail to understand why women would not like it. But I consider such men to be the exception, rather than the rule. Given that the typical case is one of a man who would not enjoy being a moral subordinate in sex, what is the prevailing sexual ideology in our culture that might account for the divergent ways in which men and women think about sex objectification? What makes being a male sex object a thrill instead of a degradation? Are there ever any circumstances where men might make the same sorts of complaints women do? Some of the clues to answering these and similar questions may be found by looking at the reactions of the female sex objects in our original example.

Notice, for instance, that the free spirit felt threatened by her objectifiers; she was not sure what they really wanted from her, and she knew that even a smile might be used as an invitation to rape. However, the sexual ideology of heterosexual men typically does not include what I shall call a "rape mentality." Men are typically physically stronger than women; therefore in a society that equates physical strength and size with power, men are typically less afraid of being overpowered in a physical attack on their bodies. Also, men need an erection to be "raped" (engulfed?) by a woman's vagina; therefore, it is more difficult for women simply to take their sexual pleasure from men whenever they feel like it. Furthermore, the sort of language we use to talk about sex suggests we simply do not have the same conception of men being harmed in sex as we do women. Men "screw" women or "fuck" women; they also tell their enemies to "fuck off" or "screw themselves." The expression "screw you" or "up yours" suggests that we can convey our hostility toward others by suggesting that they take up the female role in sex relative to us.[59] The stereotypic male is not the sort of person who can be harmed in sex, or even harmed in unwanted sex. And our language suggests that we do not even think of men as being harmed in this way. Indeed, such a conception may have its foundations in physical realities.

Furthermore, a case can be made, especially if one consults the historical literature on the subject,[60] that there is less sex that is unwanted sex for men than there is for women. First, men have traditionally not been punished, or punished as severely as women have been, for sexual transgressions. The adulterous male may have been ostracized from his community for his offense, but the adulterous female was often stoned to death.[61] Furthermore, it is the woman who must bear the burden of any absence of birth control, since it is she who becomes pregnant and who must bear any physical pain, guilt, anxiety, or social ostracism for being a single unwed mother, whether she ultimately raises the child herself or not. Furthermore, we do not have the same conception of men as being humiliated in sex as we do with women. While men may be as concerned to keep their private parts private or their intimate relations intimate as women are, sex does not prostitute a man or make him dirty or lower him on the social register in the way it can with women in our culture. Sex has been a way a woman could lose her self-respect; it can make her feel that, as a sexual being, she is a lower-class entity of an already inferior type. A stranger's sexual approach will then be viewed by a woman as a source of humiliation in a way it would not be for a man.

B. The Female Submissive Mentality

In fact, the stereotype of men in sex is that no sex is unwanted, because sex is renewed proof of a man's masculinity, that is, (in chauvinistic translation) his personhood. Sex means self-assurance and success (witness "winning the hand of the fair maid"); when a man can perform sexually he is "potent," i.e. powerful, masterful, in control. Sex for the stereotypic male means showing that he is capable of demanding and exercising the rights to well-being and freedom that make him the moral equal of other men and the moral subordinator of women. Such a stereotype suggests that a man will look upon his female boss's offer for promotion in exchange for sex as a promotion plus a bonus (instead of an intolerable means of promotion, as did the assistant manager), since, in his mind, sex is not a means to his subordination at all. Or, if he sees it as a kind of domination, or if he is physically repulsed by his boss, he is more likely than a woman to chalk it up to a "new sexual experience." At the very least, his submission is not looked upon by him as a *permanent condition.*

The fact is that in our culture, not only do men typically escape the burden of a rape mentality; they are also typically unaccustomed to adopting any sort of *submissive* mentality in sex.[62] Men chase; women retreat. Men press; women submit. It is the man who is stereotyped as the aggressive initiator of the sexual encounter, while women are their passive, reluctant, ultimately subordinate partners. It is the threatening, unscrupulous, manipulative woman who would use her passive allure to "get men where she wants them." It is the virile, successful man who gets women to do what he wants them to. "They want it anyway" or "They don't want it, so I have to take it from them if I want any" are the two most extreme justifications for male supremacy in sex. Even female-oriented pornography pictures men dominating women. Women are strapped to beds, pressed against shower doors, or posed as passively waiting for their men to come and take control.[63] It will typically not occur to a man to think that being sexy is demeaning when what sex symbolizes for him is a way of dominating his situation and his partner in it. While for many men, the expectations on performance, competition, and control in sex can be as role restrictive as the subordinate roles for women in sex the nature of the stereotype itself is one that is more favorable to their status as persons, or at least to their status as moral superiors to the women around them.

Furthermore, in those cases where women can force their hands, for example in cases of sexual harassment where the economic power is in a woman's hands, men are typically less willing to submit to any undesirable conditions than their female counterparts. Since female domination is not the *status quo,* men carry with them a kind of culturally-reinforced indignation at having to submit to what is an anomaly in the power relations of their society. Such men expect women to acquiesce to their demands, not *vice versa.* And as we suggested earlier, such expectations can become self-fulfilling prophesies, so that the instances in which men do confront dominating women are relatively rare.

C. The Homosexual Mentality

The claim is that men typically have neither a rape mentality nor a submissive mentality in their attitudes about sex. However, in the case of homosexual male relations, at least some male sex partners do have just such a mentality. The reason for this is that in at least some male homosexual relations, one partner adopts what is regarded as a stereotypical feminine role. He may walk or gesture in an effeminate manner, or he may dress in women's clothes and wear women's make-up.[64] And in sex, his role is that of passive recipient of the partner's penis. To take up a stereotypic feminine role is to take up the culture's sexual ideology of the feminine, an ideology that includes the rape mentality and the submissive mentality sketched above. And although one need not take up the ideology in full, there is ample evidence that sectors of the homosexual community do adopt just such a mentality.[65]

Similarly, if one's partner were to adopt the larger social roles generated by the heterosexual male stereotype, we could expect that partner to be the typical initiator in sex, the insertor in sex, and the dehumanizer in sex, when such dehumanization exists. The adoption of such roles tends to validate the claim that they are far from inherent in the biological nature of men and women, but constructs of a given cultural ideology.[66]

It is not uncommon for lesbians to engage in the same kind of role-playing, and so set up the kinds of power relations in sex conducive to sex objectification and reflective of typical female sex objectification.[67] However, some psychologists suggest that lesbian relations are typically less variable, more stable monogamous relations than those of their male counterparts.[68] One suggestion is that such women, while rejecting a heterosexual lifestyle and much of the stereotypic feminine role, have not taken up the kind of masculine mentality that regards sex as a vehicle for asserting one's power, domination, and superiority. Such a mentality, as we have seen, is one that shies away from intimacy, and in fact creates the expectation of a sexual relationship that is short-lived and performance oriented. Another suggestion is that women have been known to turn to other women for sex when they are dissatisfied with the subordination they confront in their male relationships.[69]

On the other hand, lesbians have also been known to adopt the kind of masculine role that is such a complete rejection of the feminine role, that men become intellectual companions and other women become sex objects.[70] Although the independent and competitive spirit of the masculine mentality need not involve sex objectification, the title of aggressor, initiator, even dominator in sex that the masculine sexual role confers is extremely conducive to the role of dehumanizer in the sexual relations of any person who adopts that role. At least, it is more conducive to such relations than is a submissive mentality.

One problem that the lesbian faces that gay men (and heterosexual women) do not, is that, since women are the notorious victims of sex objectification, lesbians are more frequently approached than their male counterparts by persons whose very sex has little or no sex appeal for them. Thus, the lesbian, more often than gay men, and in a way different from heterosexual women, may find it irritating not only that men would presume that she likes being leered at, but that she is sexually interested in men of any sort. We pointed to some of the difficulties that accompany any claims that persons not think about us in certain ways in Chapter I, section 4. However, a case could be made for demanding that persons not act toward us in ways which automatically presume we fit a certain category, when that presumption impinges on the basic right to self-determination all persons share. A right against such presumptions can then be seen as a correlary or subsidiary right to this more basic right. Thus, if male heterosexual expectations can be shown to keep the lesbian from freely pursuing a homosexual lifestyle, such expectations will constitute a moral rights violation. A woman will be assumed heterosexual by a man who lives in a culture defined by a male heterosexual power structure and for whom a woman's sexual subordination to men is a symbol of that power. The male sex objectifier's apparent rejection of a woman's status as a lesbian represents to her the kind of attitude that any man who finds heterosexual sex a symbol of his own potency can be expected to entertain. In assuming she is a potential bolster for this symbol, the male sex objectifier throws into graphic relief his sexual arrogance and sense of sexual domination.

Sexism in homosexual sex objectification might be less common than its heterosexual counterpart, but not unheard of. The reason for the suggestion that it might be less common is that male or female homosexuals would essentially have to discriminate against their own sex in such a way that would amount to placing themselves in subordinate roles along with those of their same sex. A homosexual male may have sexist attitudes about women, but these attitudes place him in a position of moral superiority over women. Any sex objectification of his male lovers that involved sexist attitudes toward them would mean treating himself (one of the same sex) on the same level of moral inequality as his partner, unless he makes an exception in his own case. Also, homosexuals need not adopt any stereotypic sex roles in order to treat one another as sex objects. Moreover, when homosexuals do adopt such roles, they need not treat each other as sex objects. The claim is only that such role-playing can be conducive to sex objectification and that we should expect the feminine partner to be the object of such treatment, when it does occur.

D. Male Sex Objects are Not Sexual Subordinates

What the above considerations suggest is that sex is a less effective vehicle for dehumanizing men than it is for women. Men typically have no rape mentality; sex does not threaten them or harm them in the way it can women. And in general, men typically have no submissive mentality in sex; indeed, they live in a society that fosters independence and dominance and in which the conventionally valued social, economic, and political status all but require such traits. Sex makes boys into men; sex does not make men dirty or make them feel humiliated. In fact, such is the power of our culture's sexual ideology that women are only beginning to believe themselves capable of the sex objectification of men on a broad social scale. Bars with male exotic dancers, sexual harassment by female employers, and even books on what to look for in a man's buttocks[71] are indicative of current trends in what women regard as their sex objectification of men.

However, even if women may be capable of thinking of men as their sexual subordinates, the claim here is that the strength of the society's sexual ideology makes it difficult, if not impossible, for women successfully to use a man's sexuality to violate his rights to well-being and freedom. A woman typically does not threaten a man in sex, and so seldom harms him in the way she can be harmed. It is more difficult for her to make him feel humiliated or lose his sense of self-respect when sex is the very thing that can give him a feeling of mastery and confidence. She may less easily or casually exploit him in sex if sex is the sort of activity that gives him the advantage, success, and status in society's eyes. And she typically will not be able to inhibit his freedom of movement or expression in her sexual relations with him if sex is a symbol of his freedom to subordinate his partner to his sexual demands. If a man takes a woman's attempts to objectify him sexually as an invitation to objectify her, it is because he does not acknowledge any other position other than that of dominator of the sexual encounter. His society's sexual ideology reinforces his rights to well-being and freedom in his sexual relations, while making it difficult for a woman to exercise hers. As a result, men do not, indeed cannot, have the same reaction to being whistled at that women do. For a man to be whistled at is not to be dehumanized, but to be labeled a he-man, macho, strong, potent. It is to enjoy the knowledge that one can demand a level of well-being and freedom that is equal to some and superior to many. Women should therefore not be surprised when men enjoy being treated as sex objects in the bars, streets, and magazines of our culture, because such men are not in fact being treated as *bona fide* sex *objects* at all. They are being treated as sexually attractive (and so mature, virile, and confident) human beings or persons.

Because women are less successful, if not unsuccessful, at treating men as sex objects (or at least at treating them the way *they* are treated), the belief that current male sex objectification is simply giving to men what women have been taking for years is a mistaken one. In fact, women who complain about their own sex objectification do more harm to their own cause by continuing to attempt to treat men as sex objects. For their attempts only give tacit approval to the phenomenon as a whole. Since their sex objectification of men is unsuccessful at dehumanizing men while men's sex objectification of them continues to succeed, the *status quo* not only continues but is reinforced by their failed attempts. When women do succeed in using sex as a vehicle for the dehumanization of men, they have been able to place themselves in some sort of position of dominance and power, either psychological or social, over those men. One should expect that as such positions increase in frequency, men will find more in their sex objectification to complain about.

A final asymmetry worth pointing out is that when women do succeed in treating men as sex objects in contemporary society, they typically do not load their sex objectification with sexist attitudes about the proper role of men as their sexual subordinates. The simple reason for this is that it is not part of our culture's sexual ideology that men be treated as sex objects. Therefore, women are not convinced, much less indoctrinated, by their sexual ideology to see men as a class as the proper sex objects of women. A woman may think that men, in virtue of the fact that they are male, in some sense deserve to be the sexual subordinates of women. Thus, she may structure her sexual relations with men around those whom she feels she can dominate or control. However, such sexism, or "reverse" sexism as it is sometimes called, is a much less common or overt feature of our society than the classic male sexism against women. Indeed, the term "sexism" is itself male-centered, since the part of the sexist is typically played by a man.[72] If women do succeed in subordinating men, or if they even care to try, they are motivated less often by an attitude toward men generally, than by a desire to treat a *particular* man as a sex object. However, one working hypothesis of this entire discussion has been that to violate intentionally the rights to well-being and freedom of another human or even to conceive of another as less deserving than other persons of those rights, without special justification, is a moral wrong that no one should commit, whether in response to a history of one's own dehumanization or not. The question of what can or should count as such justification is the topic of Chapter IV.

5. FINAL CHARACTERIZATION OF SEX OBJECTIFICATION

In light of the above considerations, our final characterization of sex objectification reads as follows: person A treats person B as a sex object, A = B or A ≠ B, if and only if three conditions hold: (1) A dehumanizes B in some context C of A's sexual relations with B or B's sexual relations with some other person D; A's dehumanization of B in C implies that A either causes B to be like an object or treats B as if B were an object in a way which violates or rejects in a *prima facie* inappropriate manner one or more of B's rights to well-being and freedom in C; (2) A values B in C solely or primarily in terms of B's instrumental ability to sexually attract, stimulate, or satisfy A or D; and (3) B's ability to sexually attract A or D as described in (2) is both the source and the means for A's dehumanization of B described in (1). In the first section, the claim was that there are specific mores and taboos that we associate with sex and sexual relations generally. It was argued that we typically place a premium in sex on some of the very rights and ideals that the dehumanization of a person either violates or rejects. Thus, the fact that the dehumanization we are concentrating on occurs in one's sexual relations with others (indeed one's sexuality is the vehicle for same) is a fact which makes this sort of dehumanization especially significant, given the significance of the sexual mores and taboos in this culture. And this dehumanization may be more objectionable than in other areas of personal relations where the rights and ideals denied in dehumanization are not placed at such a premium.

In the second section, it was suggested that a man's sex objectification of a woman is typically, although not always, an instance of sexist treatment, and it was argued that the sex stereotypes involved in the sexist attitudes and practices in sexual relations between men and women engender certain role expectations for both sexes that can be both unfavorable and restrictive of each sex. Moreover, we gave some reasons for why someone might consent to her or his own sex objectification by others. The suggestion was also made that, given the sorts of deeply-entrenched role expectations of our sexual ideology, an ideology that labels women as the proper sexual subordinates of men, we might want to say that part of the burden of moral responsibility for acting out that ideology lays outside the agent; however, in those instances where a non-culpable ignorance, intimidation, coercion and the like cannot be shown, the remainder of the burden falls on those who are in the position to choose otherwise.

The third section elucidated the claim that to act toward oneself as a sex object is to waive one's rights to well-being and freedom, an act equivalent to permitting others to treat one as a sex object if they so wish. It was stipulated that such permission may be justified only on the same kinds of grounds which are used to justify the principle of moral equality. Thus, the principle can be consistently held, in spite of one's waiving or overriding the rights to well-being and freedom guaranteed by the principle, if such justification can be found.

Finally, we suggest that sex typically is not as effective a vehicle for the dehumanization of men as it is for women. This fact helps explain why it is that men so often seem to enjoy their purported sex objectification: they are typically not successfully treated as sexual subordinates by women at all. Homosexual men may be more effectively subordinated by other homosexual men if they adopt the feminine ideology that dictates adopting the role of sex objects for men. Lesbians may sustain more stable sexual relations than their male counterparts, when they fail to structure their sexual relationships around the kind of dominant/submissive theme that can militate against affection or intimacy between the partners. We are now in a position to examine alternative conceptions of sex objectification that other philosophers have offered, in order to clarify further the nature of and objections to sex objectification.

NOTES

1 However, the setting may make all the difference. The office of an unfamiliar doctor may still be an appropriate setting for a relative stranger to scrutinize one's "private parts." And the artist's studio or nudist colony are places where consent to being watched in the nude by persons one is not intimate with is either commonplace or the *status quo*. Yet the appropriateness of the setting seems tied more to the particular cultural mores of one's community than to one's consent in that setting. So, for example, the Victorian doctor was not thought to be behaving properly if he examined more than what could be seen above bedclothes or nightgown. And some persons today find nudist colonies appalling even though the colonists consent to act as they do.

2 *See* Richard Wasserstrom, "Privacy: Some Arguments and Assumptions" in *Philosophical Law: Authority, Equality, Adjudication, Privacy,* ed. Richard Bronaugh (Westport, Connecticut: Greenwood Press, 1978), pp. 152ff.

3 *See* Charles Fried, *An Anatomy of Values: Problems of Personal and Social Choice.* (Cambridge, Massachusetts: Harvard University Press, 1970), Chapter IX.

4 *See* Wasserstrom, in Bronaugh, *op. cit.,* p. 156.

5 *See* Richard Dawkins, *The Selfish Gene* (Oxford: Oxford University Press, 1976), Chapter 9; *also see* Edward O. Wilson, *On Human Nature* (Cambridge, Massachusetts: Harvard University Press, 1978), Chapter 6.

6 *See* Sigmund Freud, *Civilization and Its Discontents,* trans. and ed. James Strachey (New York: W. W. Norton & Company, 1961), Chapter II.

7 *See* Saint Augustine, *City of God,* trans. Philip Levine (Cambridge, Massachusetts: Harvard University Press, 1966), Chapter 4.

8 *See* Reay Tannehill, *Sex in History* (New York: Stein & Day, 1980), Chapter 3.

9 I have drawn heavily for this section on the work of Ann Garry in "Pornography and Respect for Women," *Philosophy and Women,* ed. Sharon Bishop and Marjorie Weinzweig (Belmont, California: Wadsworth Publishing Co., 1979), pp. 134–135. *See also* my critique of her analysis of the relationship between sex, harm, and dehumanization, *infra,* Chapter III, section 3.

10 *See,* for example, Martin Luther "The Natural Place of Women" in *Sexual Love and Western Morality,* ed. D. P. Verene (New York: Harper Torchbooks, Harper & Row, 1972), pp. 134–143. For the Hebrew roots of this tradition *see* Tannehill, *op. cit.,* pp. 62ff.

11 For some documentation of the social, political, and economic oppression of women in contemporary society, *see* Sandra L. Bem and Daryl J. Bem, "Homogenizing the American Woman: The Power of an Unconscious Ideology" in *Feminist Frameworks,* ed. Alison Jaggar and Paula Rothenberg Struhl (New York: McGraw-Hill, 1978), pp. 6–22. For a detailed analysis of the patriarchal nature of our society and the subordinate place of women in it (including the place of male chivalry), *see* Kate Millett, *Sexual Politics* (New York: Ballantine Books, 1969), pp. 35–81.

12 Garry, *op. cit.,* p. 134.

13 Some examples of women's dehumanization in spheres other than the sexual are offered *infra* Chapter IV, section 3.

14 For a discussion of the thesis that the sexuality of women expresses an inequality in social power, see Catharine MacKinnon, "Feminism, Marxism, Method, and the State: An Agenda for Theory," *Signs: Journal of Women in Culture and Society* 7, No. 3 (Spring, 1982). "The substantive principle governing the authentic politics of women's personal lives is pervasive powerlessness to men, expressed and reconstituted daily as sexual. To say that the personal is political means that gender as a division of power is discoverable and verifiable through women's intimate experience of sexual objectification. . .", p. 535.

15 For more on our culture's sexual role expectations for women, *see infra* Chapter II, section 2B.

16 Interestingly enough, the thesis that sex promotes self-development can be used to justify both sexual promiscuity and sexual monogamy. *See* Frederick Elliston, "In Defense of Promiscuity" in *Philosophy and Sex,* ed. Robert Baker and Frederick Elliston (Buffalo, New York: Prometheus Books, 1975, pp. 234ff., and Pope Paul VI "from Humanae Vitae (1964)" in *Today's Moral Problems,* ed. Richard Wasserstrom (New York: Macmillan Publishing Company, 1975), p. 236. On the one hand "experiment and diversity" in sex is the key toward (autonomous) self-fulfillment (Elliston, p. 234); on the other hand, sexual monogamy ". . . preserves in its fullness the sense of true mutual love and its ordination toward man's most high calling to parenthood." (Pope Paul VI, p. 236).

17 Elliston, *op. cit.,* p. 235.

18 This general description of a so-called "androgynous" society is consistent with the two forms of androgyny cited by Joyce Trebilcot in "Two Forms of Androgynism," *"Femininity," "Masculinity," and "Androgyny"* ed. Mary Vetterling-Braggin (Totowa, New Jersey: Littlefield, Adams & Co., 1982), pp. 161–169. One form encourages a single

ideal, that is the combining of the virtues of the so-called masculine and feminine traits in a single person; the other ideal allows a variety of lifestyle options, ranging from what would today be called a typically "feminine" model to a purely "masculine" one. For an incisive critique of the ways in which theorizing about androgyny may only reinforce the prevailing view of the appropriateness or naturalness of sex-assigned traits, *see* Mary Anne Warren, "Is Androgyny the Answer to Sex Stereotyping?" in Mary Vetterling-Braggin, *op. cit.,* pp. 170–186.

19 This likelihood is one reason for claiming that "the personal is political." Indeed, Catharine MacKinnon believes that sex objectification is "the primary process of the subjection of women." *See* her *Signs* article, *op. cit.,* p. 541. For the ways in which that subjection enters into our language about sex *see* Robert Baker, "Sex and Language" and Janice Moulton, "Sex and Reference" in Bishop and Weinzweig, *op. cit.,* pp. 100–108.

20 For some idea of the variety of sexists and sexism that exist, *see* Marilyn Frye, "Male Chauvinism: A Conceptual Analysis" in Bishop and Weinzweig, *op. cit.,* pp. 26–28. The person who holds sexist beliefs on the basis of what he mistakenly takes to be *a priori* truths, here referred to as beliefs "without sufficient evidence", Marilyn Frye calls the "primitive" sexist. Her "doctrinaire" sexist mistakenly takes his beliefs to be based on sound evidence of some kind, confirmable in principle, if not in fact. His evidence according to the feminist, however, is not verifiable either in principle or in fact. Also notice that while the behavior of someone might be considered sexist in the absence of accompanying sexist beliefs (for example, out of unthinking habit), neither Frye nor I consider the practitioner to *be* sexist. As Frye claims in a footnote, p. 27, "this might be seen as an instance when we condemn the sin but not the sinner." However, the practitioner's moral responsibility for unreflectively acting in this manner may be another story. *See infra,* Chapter II, section 2E.

21 For the importance of this larger social context to an examination of sexism, *see* Richard Wasserstrom, "Racism and Sexism" in his *Philosophy and Social Issues* (Notre Dame, Indiana: Univesity of Notre Dame Press, 1980), p. 20.

22 The logical features here described apply *mutatis mutandis* to the concepts of female chauvinism and sexism against men, even if the pervasiveness and harm done by male chauvinism does not.

23 Jacqueline Fortunata emphasizes the offense of de-individualization in her treatment of sex objectification, part of a general description of a normative theory of sexuality in "Masturbation and Women's Sexuality," *Philosophy of Sex,* ed. Alan Soble (Totowa, New Jersey: Littlefi, ld, Adams & Co., 1980), p. 397. *Also see* Elizabeth Eames in "Sexism and Woman as Sex Object," *Journal of Thought 11,* No. 2 (April, 1976), p. 141. She says a sex object is ". . . taken as a thing to be used sexually and then discarded or put on the shelf, that is, equivalent to any object that can be used to satisfy a sexual need." *See* my criticisms of Eames, *infra* Chapter III, section 1.

24 For a critique of some of the biological arguments for the subordination of women, *see* Anne Dickason, "Anatomy and Destiny: The Role of Biology in Plato's View of Women" in *Women and Philosophy,* ed. Carol C. Gould and Marx W. Wartofsky (New York: Capricorn Books, G. P. Putnam's Sons, 1976), pp. 45–53. For a critique of some of the social and psychological arguments, *see* Joyce Trebilcot, "Sex Roles: The Argument from Nature" and Naomi Weisstein, "Psychology Constructs the Female" in *Sex Equality,* ed. Jane English (Englewood Cliffs, New Jersey: Prentice-Hall, 1977), pp. 121–129, 205–215.

25 This is the view that seems to be adopted by Richard Wasserstrom in "Racism and Sexism," *op. cit.,* pp. 40ff.

26 *See* Thomas E. Hill, Jr.'s book review of Richard Wasserstrom's *Philosophy and Social Issues, UCLA Law Review* 28, No. 1 (October, 1980), pp. 14ff. *Also see* Robert Young, "Autonomy and Socialization," *Mind* 89, No. 356 (October, 1980), pp. 565–576; and

Francine Rainone and Janice Moulton, "Sex Roles and the Sexual Division of Labor," in Mary Vetterling-Braggin, *op. cit.*, pp. 227ff.

27 For the particular ways in which such role expectations affect lesbians, *see infra,* Chapter II, section 4.

28 Then when women do use sex to gain favors, men belittle them as crafty promoters taking unfair advantage of their male counterparts, beguiling the unwitting (and therefore innocent) man into their sexual net. They are also attacked by the men with whom they may compete for using a means for securing benefits unavailable to them.

29 *See* Sandra Lee Bartky, "On Psychological Oppression" in *Philosophy and Women,* ed. Sharon Bishop and Marjorie Weinzweig (Belmont, California: Wadsworth Publishing Company, 1979), p. 35: "Suppose that I, the victim of some stereotype, believe in it myself—for why should I not believe what everyone else believes? . . . It is hard enough for me to determine what sort of person I am or ought to try to become without being shadowed by an alternate self, a truncated and inferior self that I have, in some sense, been doomed to be all the time."

30 For the effects that a dependence on physical beauty has for women, *see* Linda Phelps, "Mirror, Mirror" and Zoe Moss, "It Hurts to be Alive and Obsolete" in Jaggar and Struhl, *op. cit.*, pp. 51–56. *Also see* Dana Densmore, "On the Temptation to Be a Beautiful Object" in *Female Liberation: History and Current Politics,* ed. Roberta Salper (New York: Alfred A. Knopf, 1972).

31 *See* Sandra Lee Bartky, *op. cit.*, p. 38. *Also see,* Betty Friedan, *The Feminine Mystique* (New York: Dell Publishing Company, 1963), Chapter II and Lucy Komisar, "The Image of Woman in Advertising" in *Woman in Sexist Society,* ed. Vivian Gornick and Barbara K. Moran (New York: Basic Books, 1971), pp. 304–317.

32 This is equivalent to saying that sex roles are unjustified because they perpetuate the unfair subordination of women to men. For a defense of this thesis, *see* Rainone and Moulton's "Sex Roles and the Sexual Division of Labor" in Mary Vetterling-Braggin, *op. cit.*, pp. 229ff.

33 *See* Marc Feigen Fasteau, *The Male Machine* (New York: Dell Publishing Company, 1975), Chapter 1. "Incompetence in personal relationships is the inevitable result of belief in the masculine ideal . . ." (p. 3). ". . . it was the fear of emotions associated with being vulnerable . . . that was somehow cutting myself off from all but a narrow range of human contact." (p. 5)

34 *See* Jack Nichols, *Men's Liberation: A New Definition of Masculinity* (New York: Penguin Books, 1975). *Also see* Fasteau, *op. cit.*, Chapter 3.

35 *See* Fasteau, *op. cit.*, Chapter 2. *Also see* Michael Korda, *Male Chauvinism! How It Works* (New York: Ballantine Books, 1973), Chapter 3.

36 Of course, this choice may actually be less free than she believes if she has chosen to strip in response to the subtle psychological intimidation or indoctrination of her culture's sexual ideology. *See infra,* Chapter II, section 2B.

37 *See* Elizabeth L. Beardsley's account of the conditions for blameworthiness and praiseworthiness from the perspective of moral worth in "Determinism and Moral Perspectives," *Philosophy and Phenomenological Research* 21, No. 1 (September, 1960), pp. 1–20. For an analysis of the relation between moral responsibility and blame *see* Joel Feinberg, "Action and Responsibility" in *Doing and Deserving* (Princeton, New Jersey: Princeton University Press, 1970), pp. 127ff.

38 Such speculations can be inferred from Dawkins' chapter on the sexes, *op. cit.*, pp. 151–178.

39 *See* Dorothy Dinnerstein, *The Mermaid and the Minotaur* (New York: Harper Colophon Books, Harper & Row, 1976), esp. Chapters 6 and 7. *Also see* Nancy Chodorow, *The Reproduction of Mothering* (Berkeley and Los Angeles, California: University of California Press, 1978), Part II.

40 *See* Beardsley, *op. cit.*, pp. 16ff. for the sense of "ultimate moral equality" which such determinism suggests.

41 *See* Beardsley, *op. cit.*, pp. 3ff. in explanation of the view of the reconciling or "soft" determinist, who would reconcile free will with determinism.

42 For a detailed discussion of the various ways in which feminists interpret the notion of sex equality, *see* Alison Jaggar, "On Sexual Equality," in *Sex Equality*, ed. Jane English (Englewood Cliffs, New Jersey: Prentice-Hall Publishing Co., 1977), pp. 93–109.

43 *See* Elizabeth Beardsley, "Moral Worth and Moral Credit," *The Philosophical Review* 66 (July, 1957), pp. 304–328.

44 Jacqueline Fortunata emphasizes the single participant in her definition of masturbation in "Masturbation and Women's Sexuality" in Soble, *op. cit.*, pp. 390ff.

45 D. P. Verene describes Kant's attitudes toward sex and marriage, in *Sexual Love and Western Morality*, ed. D. P. Verene (New York: Harper & Row, 1972), p. 91. *Also see* his chapter on Kant discussing "Duties to the Body and Crimes against Nature," pp. 160ff.

46 Thomas Aquinas on "The Divinity of Marriage," in Verene, *op. cit.*, pp. 120ff.

47 Sigmund Freud on "The Sex Instinct and Human Happiness," in Verene, *op. cit.*, p. 220.

48 There may very well be a (hetero)sexual bias implicit in these judgments. If so, I apologize, and explain my predominant interest in such cases in terms of it.

49 *See* Bartky, *op. cit.*, p. 38; *also see* Densmore, *op. cit.*

50 *See* Herbert Morris, "Persons and Punishment" in Wasserstrom's *Today's Moral Problems*, *op. cit.*, pp. 318ff.

51 *See*, for example, Judith Tormey's "Exploitation, Oppression, and Self-Sacrifice" in Gould and Wartofsky, *op. cit.*, p. 215. Tormey argues that to consent to one's own exploitation is wrong because one creates an opportunity for someone to do something wrong.

52 *Cf.* Tormey, *op. cit.:* "In short, to freely accept being exploited is to encourage selfishness. To encourage selfishness is to do something wrong. Therefore, the exploitee in such cases is an appropriate target of moral censure." (p. 215)

53 *Cf.* Tormey, *op. cit.* When one consents to one's own exploitation and this relation continues, "habits of expectation or traits of character may arise which will carry over into the exploiter's relations with others. They will be expected to acquiesce in the same unfair balance of benefits and burdens the exploiter has come to take for granted from the willing submission to exploitation experienced in the relation in question." (p. 215)

54 Mary Vetterling-Braggin argues along similar lines in her discussion of women's participation in traditionally all-male sports programs in the *Journal of Philosophy of Sport* 8 (1981).

55 *See* Hill's book review of Wasserstrom's *Philosophy and Social Issues op. cit.*, p. 143. *Also see* Francine Rainone and Janice Moulton, "Sex Roles and the Sexual Division of Labor," in Mary Vetterling-Braggin, *op. cit.*, pp. 227ff.

56 *See* R. S. Downie and Elizabeth Telfer's review of the Kantian notion of respect for persons in Chapter I of their book *Respect for Persons* (London: Allen & Unwin, 1969), pp. 13–37. *Also see* Immanuel Kant, *The Metaphysical Principles of Virtue*, trans. James Ellington (New York: Bobbs-Merrill Company, 1964), Part II, sections 37–41; and David Gauthier, *Practical Reasoning* (Oxford: Oxford University Press, 1963), pp. 119ff; *see* John Rawls, *A Theory of Justice* (Cambridge, Massachusetts: Harvard University Press, 1971), pp. 337ff for various discussions of the meaning and importance of respect for persons in a theory of right conduct.

57 Gregory Vlastos, "Justice and Equality" in *Social Justice*, ed. Richard B. Brandt (Englewood Cliffs, New Jersey: Prentice-Hall, 1962), p. 40.

58 Compare the deferential wife in Thomas E. Hill's article, "Servility and Self-Respect" in Wasserstrom's *Today's Moral Problems, op. cit.,* p. 139. *Also see infra,* Chapter IV, section 1A.

59 *See* Robert Baker, " 'Pricks and 'Chicks': A Plea for Persons", esp. pp. 57–63 and Janice Moulton, "Sex and Reference", esp. pp. 34–38 in Baker and Elliston, *op. cit. Also see* Stephanie Ross, "How Words Hurt: Attitudes, Metaphors and Oppression" in *Sexist Language,* ed. Mary Vetterling-Braggin (Totowa, New Jersey: Littlefield, Adams & Co., 1981), pp. 194–213.

60 *See,* e.g., Reay Tannehill, *Sex in History* (New York: Stein and Day, 1980) and Denis deRougemont, *Love in the Western World* (New York: Harper and Row, 1956, revised edition 1974).

61 *See* Tannehill, *op. cit.,* pp. 62ff.

62 For some insight into what the burden of a woman's rape consciousness entails, *see* Susan Griffin, "Rape: The All-American Crime" in *Feminism and Philosophy* ed. Mary Vetterling-Braggin, Frederick A. Elliston, and Jane English (Totowa, New Jersey: Littlefield, Adams, & Co., 1978), pp. 313–332. *Also see* Pamela Foa, "What's Wrong with Rape" specifically pp. 354ff in Vetterling-Braggin, Elliston, and English, *op. cit.* for a discussion of the correlations between a rape mentality and a stereotypic submissive mentality in heterosexual sex.

63 Interestingly enough, female-oriented pornography has not had nearly the successful distribution that its male-oriented counterparts do. One speculation is that much of what can be found in such magazines can be found in heterosexual male or homosexual male pornography instead (and since its advertising and articles would have a female orientation, the magazines would not be picked up by men). An interesting and relatively controversial thesis is that women typically do not respond erotically to visual images as much as to tactile and auditory images, to the process and not the "score" of the relationship. Men, on the other hand, typically respond to what they see, and to immediate sexual gratification. While some men respond to process and some women to immediate gratification, the argument is that since the sexes typically have such different needs, they cannot possibly be expected to respond similarly to the same kinds of sexual stimuli. And these are as much a part of a female and male "natural" tendency as they are products of a culture's sexual ideology. Those who are atypical are simply those who do not manifest this inherent tendency. Thus the fact that *Viva* (a female *Playboy*) bombed or that women either laugh or blush, but do not get aroused as a rule by male strippers is due to the different kinds of sexual stimuli they need to become aroused. *See* Beatrice Faust, *Woman Sex and Pornography* (New York: Macmillan Publishing Co., 1980). Of course, the "fact" that women are not typically turned on by male strippers would be hotly contested by thousands of women who pant, claw and scream to see their favorite studs "take it off" at one of many metropolitan club/bars. That this behavior only reinforces women's sex objectification without successfully dehumanizing men is argued *infra,* section 4D of this chapter.

64 *See* Donald Webster Cory, "Homosexuality" in *The Encyclopedia of Sexual Behavior,* Vol. 1, ed. Albert Ellis and Alber Abarbanel (New York: Hawthorn Books, 1961), pp. 488ff.

65 *See,* e.g., Peter Fisher, *The Gay Mystique* (New York: Stein and Day, 1972), pp. 68–80. *Also see* Wainwright Churchill, *Homosexual Behavior Among Males: A Cross-Cultural and Cross-Species Investigation* (New York: Hawthorn Books, 1967); and *see* Janice G. Raymond, *The Transexual Empire* (Boston: Beacon Press, 1979), esp. her introduction, pp. 1–18 and her incisive criticism of those scientists who profess to find culture, not biology, as the important determiner of male and female behavior, Chapter 2, pp. 43–68.

66 *See* Weisstein, *op. cit. Also see,* Judith M. Bardwich and Elizabeth Douvan, "Ambivalence: The Socialization of Women" in *Women in Sexist Society,* ed. Vivian Gornick

and Barbara K. Moran (New York: Basic Books, 1971), pp. 225–241; and *see* Janice G. Raymond, *op. cit.*, Chapter 2, esp. pp. 59ff.

67 *See* Leah Fritz, *Dreamers and Dealers: An Intimate Appraisal of the Women's Movement* (Boston, Massachusetts: Beacon Press, 1979), Chapter 4.

68 For example, *see* Cory in Ellis and Abarbanel, *op. cit.*, pp. 490ff.

69 *See* Bernice Goodman, *The Lesbian: A Celebration of Difference* (New York: Out and Out Books, 1977). *Also see* the Radicalesbians, "The Woman Identified Woman" in *Radical Feminism*, ed. Anne Koedt, Ellen Levine and Anita Rapone (New York: Quadrangle/NY Times Book Co., 1973).

70 *See* Fritz, *op. cit.*, p. 109.

71 *See* Christie Jenkins, *Buns: A Woman Looks at Men's* (New York: G. P. Putnam's Sons, 1980).

72 *See* Marilyn Frye, "Male Chauvinism: A Conceptual Analysis" in Bishop and Weinzweig, *op. cit.*, p. 27.

chapter 3

A Critique of the Literature

It should be clear by now that there is great variety in the kinds of sex objectification that exist, and that while some persons may have much to complain about concerning sex objectification, others may have very little. In light of these facts, the claim of this chapter is that the alternative characterizations of sex objectification previously described by professional philosophers are either *incomplete* (in that they do not capture the variety of cases that do exist) or *inaccurate* (in that they incorrectly characterize the cases they do cite) or both. On the basis of the information we have gathered from Chapters I and II, let us examine some of these alternative characterizations.

1. SEX OBJECTIFICATION AS USE, DISREGARD, AND EXPLOITATION

In her article "Sexism and Woman as Sex Object,"[1] Elizabeth Eames makes the important conceptual point that women who complain about being treated as sex objects are complaining about being treated as "sex things," not merely as "objects of sexual desire," by men.[2] Eames goes on to specify what is entailed by "being treated as a thing and not a person" by referring to the phenomenon of exploitation. She states that ". . . to treat a human being as an object . . . implies an immoral attitude of exploitation;" and she follows the term exploited in a later paragraph with the parenthetical remark "(treated as a 'thing' rather than a person)."[3] For Eames, then, to treat a person as an object is not normatively neutral; it is to treat a person as an object in ways she should be treated as a person, but is not. To use the terminology of this book, it is to dehumanize her. Dehumanization of a person on this view then implies, if it is not equivalent to, the exploitation of a person.

However, this conceptual picture becomes somewhat complicated by the further claim that prostitution is both exploitive *and* dehumanizing;[4] perhaps the aim here is to emphasize the exploitive element of prostitution as well as to define it as a form of sex objectification, viz. as a dehumanizing process. Eames most clearly delineates her sense of dehumanization when she states that sex objects are in the situation ". . . of being used, exploited, of having their feelings, desires, or interests disregarded, in short, of being treated as things rather than as persons."[5] Again she speaks as if dehumanization somehow implies exploitation; yet here she also adds the notions of "'use" and "disregard" of sentiments. Such terms, we can assume, carry negative normative weight; otherwise they would not be used to describe what Eames sees as a morally objectionable act.[6] In fact, other philosophers' discussions of the meaning of the term "exploitation" suggest that Eames is in effect further defining what she sees as the exploitative component of sex objectification, rather than adding any independent conceptual information to it. Judith Tormey, for example, suggests that to exploit a person is to *use* that person for the express purpose of gaining some advantage for oneself or others at the expense of the person used. Exploitation usually carries with it a negative normative component, since it often implies a *prima facie* inappropriate *disregard* for the interests of the exploited.[7] However, as Tormey points out, the problem is not necessarily one of ignoring the exploitee's interests, but rather implies taking them into account, only to fail to give them their proper weight.[8] While such refinements do not seem to detract significantly from Eames' discussion, the main issue would appear to be whether or not sex objectification, indeed any form of dehumanization, necessarily constitutes the exploitation of the object. In response to Eames, then, we could argue that while it is typical for the sex objectifier to use the sex object for a turn-on at the expense of her privacy or self-determination (especially recall the assistant manager here), the sex objectifier may dehumanize his object out of simple malice or to express the principle that all women of a certain sort are sex objects or merely to show her who is boss. Such actions entail using a woman's sexuality as the vehicle for her dehumanization, but they do not entail her inappropriate use by others for personal profit or gain.

Furthermore, the notion of exploitation becomes even more complicated when used to describe prostitution. Eames says prostitution is an instance of exploitation because "sexual intercourse is bought and sold as a commodity" and that advertising exploits women by using female titillation and male desire "to sell products".[9] Pimps and advertisers may exploit women in the Marxist sense by making (and keeping) the profits from their labor, but Eames does not seem to be objecting to the political economy of exploitation. She does think it is in some way immoral to exploit women in the above contexts, but to describe prostitutes merely as women who are being taken advantage of in ways that give inappropriate appreciation to their own interests is too facile. At least some prostitutes and most models would say they freely consent to or permit the use of their bodies in the above ways without obvious external pressure to do so, and are often well-paid for their work. That is, many so-called "sex objects" would argue that their use in "girly magazines, strip shows [and] hard and soft core pornography" (more examples of exploitation according to Eames) is neither to their unfair disadvantage nor in wrongful disregard of their interests, and so not a form of exploitation or dehumanization at all.

If such things as prostitution and pornography in contemporary Western culture are exploitive, it is because such phenomena involve marketing the erotic appeal of women's bodies at the expense of fostering and perpetuating an unfavorable and restrictive stereotype of women as the sexual subordinates of men. It was argued in Chapter II that the stereotype is unfavorable because it labels women as the moral inferiors of men, when they are in fact the moral equals of men. The stereotype is restrictive if it fosters certain intimidating kinds of sexual role expectations for women that make it difficult for them to live self-determined lives. If there is, in heterosexual male-oriented pornography or prostitution, any "disregard" for a female sex object's interests, it is a disregard for any desire she may have to be portrayed as a moral equal in sex and a disregard for any desire she may have to live a relatively autonomous life, restricted by a minimum of the sort of role expectations that such stereotypes generate.[10]

Furthermore, although marketing women as sex objects may tend to lump women in categories that would blur their uniqueness as individuals, it would be misleading to say that the bodies to which women are reduced are always ". . . equivalent to any object which might be used to satisfy a sexual need."[11] In Chapter II, the claim was that a sex objectifier might find one and only one woman, or only one kind of woman to be the sort of woman whom he could or would regard as his sexual subordinate, and the *Playboy* centerfold with the brilliant career in physics is hardly reduced to just any sex object. Besides, one would assume that most men, sex objectifiers or not, would agree that only certain kinds of women can really "satisfy their sexual needs" and not just any woman or any female body. In any case, although Eames is on the right track in thinking that sex objectification is a kind of dehumanization, she fails to specify clearly what that dehumanization amounts to. On the one hand we are told it all but amounts to exploitation, on the other that it is exploitation *plus* some other component, since prostitution is described as both exploitive and dehumanizing. When this added component appears to be nothing other than a further refinement on the concept of exploitation, we find the refinements in need of further qualification. Also, the examples are of only limited scope. Because more cases are cited where women usually consent to being treated as sex objects than when they do not, one wonders what the notion of "disregarding a person's interests" has to do with sex objectification at all. Surely one would not readily consent to something one knew was not in one's best interests, unless coerced, deceived, and so on. But Eames does not give the impression (nor should she) that all advertising, pornography, and so on is coercive. And even if the interests referred to are the real or genuine interests of the sex object, as opposed to her perceived interests, it remains to be shown in the ways suggested above why advertising or pornography disregards these interests or what the sex object's real interests are.

Notwithstanding such criticism, Eames' article remains an important preliminary investigation into the morality of sex objectification. First, it marks the conceptual distinction between object as "thing" and object as "objective." Second, it points out that sex objectification implies treating a person as a thing. And third, it describes some of the ways in which the exploitation of women figures in many of the examples of the sex objectification of women. Chapter I of this book takes such an investigation further by noting that since there are cases where treating a person as an object is unproblematic, we can add the negative normative component we need by noting that treating a person as a sex object implies treating that person as less than a moral equal. We have analyzed why a woman might consent to her sex objectification, given our *prima facie* objections to it, and we have shown how sex stereotypes can act as restrictions on women's (and men's) autonomy, making any social conditions that reinforce those stereotypes of questionable moral value. Such additional investigation serves to account for the apparent variety of cases that exist as well as to provide the groundwork for any sustained moral objections to those cases.

2. SEX OBJECTIFICATION AS TAKING THE PART FOR THE WHOLE

A different sort of characterization of sex objectification is given by Sandra Lee Bartky in her larger discussion of psychological oppression.[12] She states that a person is sexually objectified ". . . when her sexual parts or sexual functions are separated out from the rest of her personality and reduced to the status of mere instruments, or else regarded as if they were capable of representing her".[13] She goes on to state that according to this definition, the prostitute, "the *Playboy* bunny, the female breeder and the bathing beauty" would all be victims of sex objectification. She states further that all sexual relations involve some sex objectification; the question is, what differentiates the objectionable from the unobjectionable cases? She gives her answer by referring to the habitual identification of a woman with her body in virtually every area of her experience, and gives some examples to make her point.[14]

First let us examine Bartky's characterization of sex objectification in more detail. If one's sexual parts or functions are reduced to "mere instruments," what might this reduction entail? If we interpret the expression "mere instruments" to mean "nothing more than what is specified by the term 'instruments,' " as in "a mere pittance" or "a mere two ounces," then perhaps what Bartky is suggesting is that such parts are not regarded as aesthetic objects, of intrinsic, not *instrumental* value. It was claimed at the end of Chapter I that the sex object is not an aesthetic object, since her value is in her instrumental ability to sexually stimulate or attract others. However, Bartky's bathing beauty could be seen as an aesthetic object by some admirer of feminine physique, and one's sexual parts on this reading can be treated as "mere instruments" by one's sex partner while the person with those parts is not treated as a sex object, viz. when one's parts are treated as the instruments of one's partner's stimulation at the same time one is treated as a moral equal or person with needs, desires, and preferences of one's own. It is persons who are "reduced" to mere instruments, and not the parts themselves, which can, although they do not always, act as such. Thus, the thesis of this book is that persons are treated as sex objects when they are reduced from the status of person to that of moral subordinate.

However, one can also use the term "mere" in a different sense. When the free spirit reflects that women are more than mere sex objects, or when the unhappy wife asserts that her husband treats her as nothing but an object, it was suggested that they were not complaining about being treated as objects, but complaining about not being treated as moral equals. To be treated as a 'mere' object, then, would mean to be treated as an object, but not in some other appropriate way, in this case, as a moral equal.[15] Perhaps what Bartky means is that one's sexual parts are treated as instruments, *and not in some other appropriate way.* It seems clear that an instrument used to perform a specified task can be misused or mishandled; the trick is to specify in what ways one's sexual parts are misused so as to explain why those who are treated as sex objects complain the way they do.

However, the discussion that follows the above characterization of sex objectification never directly answers this question. Instead it refers almost exclusively to the problem of "taking the part for the whole" — that is, around regarding a person "as if her sexual parts were capable of representing her."[16] But this regard constitutes only the latter half of the characterization, conceptually distinct from the former. In fact, if we assume that the "mere" in "mere instruments" has negative normative implications, then the latter part of the characterization must be distinguished from the former if Bartky's remarks about any unobjectionable sex objectification are to be consistent with her characterization of it. She goes on to discuss the woman who, without any apparent moral censure, simply wants to be conceived solely as a sexually desirable body for her sex partner. According to such a discussion, a woman's sexual parts "represent" her when a woman is valued solely for her body's (or body parts') sexual desirability. This "identification of a person with her sexuality" becomes objectionable when that identification "becomes habitually extended into every aspect of her experience."[17] Bartky is saying that valuing a woman solely for the sexual stimulus she can provide can be welcome and appropriate in some contexts, "unwelcome and inappropriate" in others. Here she notes a point about the context of the objectification that is consistent with the observations made at the beginning of Chapter I, namely that while some situations may be appropriate to initiate a sexual encounter, others may not be. However, what is still missing is an explanation of why those contexts in which the sexualization is inappropriate are indeed objectionable. Specifically which areas, one might ask, are those in which the identification of a person with her sexuality is inappropriate? To answer by citing "non-sexual relations" begs the question (*which* relations are these?). Furthermore, the case of the unhappy wife suggests that the problem with sex objectification need not be one of habitual sexualization since the unhappy wife is regarded as a brilliant defense lawyer by the very man who objectifies her in bed. While Bartky's characterization of sex objectification goes a long way toward pointing up some of the common problems with sex objectification, it falls short of explaining fully what the inappropriateness in any one context comes to.

Bartky also marks an interesting and important distinction between "separating one's sexual parts from the rest of one's personality" and "taking the [sexual] part [of a person] for the whole." Certainly a woman's gynecologist can focus her or his attention on that woman's breast in search of any malignancy without reducing the woman to a breast, i.e. valuing her solely for some part of her sexually desirable anatomy. Thus, it is clear that separating one's sexual parts from one's personality, reducing them to mere instruments, and taking them to represent the whole are three conceptually distinct phenomena. The problem then is that it is never explicitly stated as to what counts as misused or abused sexual parts. Perhaps this is because the burden of explanation in the subsequent discussion is on "taking the part for the whole," but if such a burden can be adequately lifted by the latter half of the characterization, the first part fails to perform any explanatory function. A fuller accounting of the problem with reducing body parts to "mere instruments" seems in order.

Bartky wants to distinguish between objectionable and unobjectionable cases of sex objectification, since she believes that all sexual relations involve some sex objectification and not all sexual relations are objectionable. Her reasoning is that sex is the sort of experience in which attention paid to such things as one's mathematical ability seems "absurdly out of place"; often all a woman wants is to be regarded as "nothing but a sexually intoxicating body".[18] And, according to Bartky, in the sexual tension of the moment, this is just what she becomes. Bartky then cites the existentialist tradition, Sartre in particular, as a tradition that bases sexual relations on just this sort of objectification.[19]

However, such a tradition does not in fact describe ordinary sexual relations as sex objectifying in the way characterized by Bartky. When she discusses ordinary sex and Sartrean sex, the reference is to how "the sexual part of a person is regarded as if it could represent her." According to one plausible interpretation of this phrase, she is referring to the way in which the sexually enticing *body* of a woman, as opposed to some part of her personality, is regarded by her sex partner as her sole value to him in that context. But unobjectionable Sartrean sex has been thought by several philosophers to be "complete" sex, where each partner allows him/herself to be "taken over" by an active desire, which is desire not merely for the other's body, but also a desire that one be desired by one's partner in return. Each partner's embodying desire is active and actively responsive to the other's.[20] Sartre's "double reciprocal incarnation"[21] involves more than two persons desiring each others' bodies, but also involves each desiring that the partner desire the other's body. This is the second aspect of the *double* (reciprocal) incarnation. Yet this is hardly the attitude of a man who regards his partner as if her sole value were in her (bodily) ability to excite him sexually. She is also valued as one who can (and hopefully will) desire her sex partner in return. This is not the kind of sexual value Bartky seems to address when she says the sex object's sexual parts "represent" her. And surely the partner is not treated as equivalent to the inanimate body part. Otherwise, how could the Sartrean sex partner expect any reciprocal desires at all?

Bartky mentions the sadist in her footnote as an example of truncated Sartrean sex ("incomplete" sex)[22] and states that most of her examples fall into this category. But the sadist values the sex partner solely for what harming her can do to turn him on; he does not or need not value the partner's desire that he be turned on.[23] Thus, it could be argued that only incomplete sex acts fit Bartky's characterization of sex objectification on the reading we have given it. It would, of course, be absurd for a man to pay attention to a woman's mathematical ability in the sex act. But not paying attention to it hardly implies his regarding her sexual parts as capable of representing the whole of her, or valuing her solely for her sexuality. For to value her solely as a sexy body is to value none of the feelings, desires, or interests of the person with that body. On the contrary, not paying attention to such features as her mathematical ability is consistent with giving her feelings, desires, or interests in the sex act their *proper weight*. So, for example, Eames asks: ". . . if a man and a woman freely agree that they desire each other, if each fulfills the sexual needs of the other, if each treats the other with concern for the other's welfare and with sensitivity for the other's feelings, if their sexual experience is mutually fulfilling, is this still a case of woman as sex object . . .?"[24] In other words, taking the sexual part for the whole, which suggests inappropriate consideration for some or all of the feelings, desires, or interests of one's sex partner, is not equivalent to paying attention to a part of the whole, that, taken by itself, does not have such implications. Because only the former expression is used in the above characterization of sex objectification and because the expression "mere instruments" makes the most sense with negative moral weight attached, we cannot consistently call any case of sex objectification so characterized unobjectionable without citing exceptional circumstances. Bartky is correct in her assurances that not all sexual relations are objectionable. But once she makes them sex objectifying relations, they are inappropriate relations unless we can show otherwise.

Another problem with the above characterization of sex objectification is that the *Playboy* bunny, the female breeder, the prostitute and the bathing beauty do not strike one as obvious victims of sex objectification on such a model. The *Playboy* bunny, as we have noted, is often described as a dedicated career woman or a great tennis player, and female breeders, who one can assume are women chosen for their superior genes — genes that can encode both superior mental and physical capabilities — have more to offer their progeny (women and men) than a good body. Their bodies, therefore, are not regarded by their readers and breeders, respectively, as if they were capable of representing them as personalities. They are either valued as something more than a sexy body or their sexiness has as much to do with their minds as their bodies. Both kinds of cases appear in the examples of sex objectification listed in Chapter I of this book. The unhappy wife is valued as a diligent lawyer. The assistant manager is sexy in part because she is intelligent. Yet the characterization under criticism here suggests that if such features occur, the cases cannot be those of sex objectification. Furthermore, why must a bathing beauty have nothing more to offer than certain sexual parts? Miss America must be talented (sing, play an instrument, converse intelligently, and the like) as well as beautiful. One advantage to the characterization of sex objectification given in Chapter I is that the sex object is a sexual subordinate, one treated as lacking the sorts of rights to well-being and freedom that persons have. It is in this respect that she is treated like an object, and not with respect to her intelligence or "the rest" of her personality. Besides, someone like the construction worker or husband or company president wants someone to appreciate what he has to offer and to acknowledge his imposition on her time or recreation. Thus, dehumanization may be treating a person as less than a moral equal, but only in a way which gives *prima facie* inappropriate consideration to that person's rights to well-being and freedom. Such treatment seldom, if ever, implies valuing a person's sexuality to the exclusion of other features of her personality.

Even if the notion of taking the part to represent the whole were a more common feature of sex objectification, the contexts or circumstances in which the fragmentation occurs are important in ways Bartky does not mention. For example, it is difficult to see how the thoughtless husband could regard his wife's sexual parts as "capable of representing her" when he clearly does not regard them as capable of representing her in the courtroom. Nor does the company president, for all his sexual preoccupations, disregard his sex object's managerial abilities. Perhaps if the characterization had stated "capable of representing her in some context C of the object and objectifier's personal or sexual relations," excluding such cases might have been avoided. However, Bartky's two main examples of objectionable sex objectification are those in which the objectifiers are perfect or near-perfect strangers, pedestrians and a prospective employer, respectively. In such cases, there is no long-standing personal or professional relationship in which one might need to specify the context in which sex objectification occurs, to distinguish it from other contexts of the relationship. The characterization of sex objectification in Chapter I stipulates some context C in which the sexual relations of object and objectifier occur.

One reason why Bartky may have limited herself to such cases is that she believes, as mentioned earlier in this section, that the objections to sex objectification lie in the fact that women are often "habitu-ally" identified with their bodies "in every area" of their experience.[25] Thus, according to Bartky, when a woman objects to being treated as a sex object, she is objecting to the fact that there is no context of her per-sonal or professional life when she is not treated as a mere sexually stimulating body. The problem with this line of reasoning is that women who complain about being treated as sex objects are also typi-cally treated as sisters, mothers, and friends in other contexts of their personal experience. The unhappy wife, it was observed, was re-garded as an able lawyer, the assistant manager, a diligent employee. So the complaints cannot derive solely from such habituation. Bartky seems to clear the air by suggesting that ". . . to be routinely perceived by others in a sexual light on occasions *where such a perception is inap-propriate*"[26] (my emphasis) is the way to explain any objections to that perception. That is, it is those instances of identification of a woman with her body in "unwelcome and inappropriate" contexts where the objections arise.

But now we have come full circle: the answer to the question, "when is sex objectification inappropriate?" is "when it occurs on occasions when it is inappropriate." Bartky is caught in a dilemma: if she pins the objection on the habitual identification of a woman with her body, then she cannot explain those isolated instances in which women com-plain about being treated as sex objects when they are not so treated in other areas of their experience. In fact, some women who think that their bodies are their best asset might not even think that such a ritual identification is a bad idea. At least, or so they might think, they are appreciated for what they have. On the other hand, if the objection re-sides in defining those contexts in which the identification is "unwelcome and inappropriate," then we need some explanation as to why some contexts are inappropriate and others not. Pursuing both avenues is clearly no solution. Let us turn to the specific examples of sex objectification given by Bartky to see if they offer the distinction between objectionable and unobjectionable cases.

The first example is one of a chairman staring at a female candi-date's breasts while interviewing her for a faculty position. The inap-propriateness of the staring is described in the following terms: (1) the candidate's "wants and needs play no role in the encounter;" (2) "she is discomfited, feels humiliated, and performs badly"; and (3) "the ob-jectifying perception that splits a person into parts . . stands revealed

. . . as a way of maintaining dominance.[27] This description can be criticized on the following grounds: first, it is unclear that the candidate's wants and needs play no role at all. She wants the interview; the chairman has acceded. She wants the job; he is probably fully aware of this. What he ignores are her wishes that he not stare at her breasts. But even this may have its subtleties: he may know she does not like his staring, but he may also want to see how she can stand up under the sexual pressure she is sure to get from his male colleagues if she is hired. Furthermore, the fact that she may want a hamburger for lunch or like toy poodles plays no role in the actual interview; indeed, it would be inappropriate or surprising if such facts did. The point is that if any wants are treated inappropriately, they are given what is more accurately termed "inappropriate" weight in the chairman's deliberations; the inappropriateness is not always in that they are given no weight at all. The description refers exclusively to ignoring the candidate's sentiments (as if they did not exist); this is consistent with Bartky's claim that the chairman values the candidate solely for the bodily stimulation she can afford him. In this sense, she is "nothing more than a body." However, this is just false in many, if not most, actual cases of sex objectification.

Second, the sex object is discomfited and humiliated by the continual staring of the chairman. However, she is discomfited only because she has noticed his stare. But suppose his stare had gone unnoticed. He still regards her breasts "as if they were capable of representing her" and so can be described as harboring sex objectifying attitudes about her. But she will not feel humiliated or perform badly in the interview if she remains unaware of how he regards her. Furthermore, it is unclear how he can insure a "way of maintaining dominance" over her if his dominating stare gets no further than his own head. Or suppose that the candidate continues to perform well, despite the obvious stare, and in fact ends by confronting the chairman with his annoying habit. Here again, it is not so much that he is successful at making her "perform badly" or at "maintaining his dominance" over her, but that he would even consider doing such a thing. The point is that it is unclear from this example how much the complaint against sex objectification should rest with the objectionable practices of the objectifier (the chairman in this case) and how much of it should rest with the attitudes he takes toward his object. The characterization offered in Chapter I of this discussion suggests the wrong is not to be found (necessarily) in the reaction the sex object has to her objectifier, but in the inappropriate consideration, either in thought or practice, that the objectifier gives to the sex object's rights to well-being and freedom.

The second example is of a woman much like the free spirit, who is whistled and hooted at from a streetcorner by a group of men.[28] This case is distinguished from the first in that the elements of dominance and humiliation emerge in the act of "making her see herself as they (her objectifiers) see her." "They could, after all," she states, "have enjoyed me in silence." But what is the difference between this case and the case of the faculty chairman, other than the fact that the chairman does not verbalize his objectification? Like the men on the streetcorner, the chairman makes the candidate feel uncomfortable because he has made her aware of her own sexuality in an environment in which the subject of sex would otherwise be absent; indeed, *he has made her aware of how he sees her.* He is deBeauvoir's Self defining the Other as sexual, as subordinate, as passive object to his active subject.[29] However, Bartky talks as if it makes all the difference to how we evaluate the second case that the men did not enjoy her in silence. Yet there is no humiliation, no discomfiture that is felt in the second case that is not felt in the first. Furthermore, if the two cases are equivalent in that the sex object is made aware of her objectification, then Bartky seems to confirm our suspicions concerning the first case that it is the sex object's reactions to some sort of overt sex objectification that makes the sex objectification objectionable. At least, if the sex object has no awareness of what is going on, we have no basis for evaluating the sex objectification. We have argued that this way of evaluating sex objectification has a ring to it that is not consistent with how women often feel about how they are viewed as individuals. Even if we could be convinced that no sex objectifying attitude would ever find its way into practice, women continue to complain about being considered the sexual subordinates of men. If this is true, then even the most preliminary characterization of sex objectification should not only mark the distinction between sex objectifying attitudes and practices, but address the question of the normative status of each.

Notwithstanding the above critique, Bartky makes some important points about sex objectification worth repeating. First, the fact that Bartky uses women and not men as her examples of persons being treated as sex objects reinforces the view articulated in Chapters I and II of this book that women constitute the paradigm cases of sex objects and that, while we should acknowledge the occurrence of male sex objectification, it has profoundly different implications in contemporary Western culture for a man's social power and self-esteem. Second, the domination or subordination of the sex object plays a central role in both the more typical as well as atypical cases of sex objectification. Third, there is an important sense in which the sex object's value as a person is thought to derive solely or primarily from her instrumental ability to stimulate or satisfy men sexually, such that a variety of contexts will be judged inappropriate contexts for sexualizing her. However, as we have noted above, this is not equivalent to saying that the sex object is a person whose sexual parts are regarded as capable of representing her. Further, Bartky tries to make her characterization of sex objectification morally neutral in order to capture what she sees as unobjectionable cases when (1) the notion of "identifying the part with the whole" has clear negative implications, and when (2) the notion of "mere instruments" only makes sense with negative normative weight attached to it. The bodies in unobjectionable sex are the bodies of persons with recognized rights to well-being and freedom, not sex objectified persons whose rights to well-being and freedom are typically violated or abused. And if there is a moral difference between privately thinking of a woman as a sex object and overtly acting toward her on the basis of those thoughts, then any characterization of sex objectification should help us clarify that difference.

On the other hand, the characterization of sex objectification presented in Chapters I and II allows for the fact that persons may find sex objectifying attitudes objectionable in the absence of any objectifying practices. The exact nature of this attitude is described in terms of conceiving of a person as less than a moral equal. Chapter II includes an analysis of the humiliation the sex object may feel in terms of the invasion of her sexual privacy and of the presence of certain Victorian sexual mores. This sort of humiliation is then contrasted with the way the male sex object may feel. Furthermore, the proposed analysis of sex objectification accounts for the many cases in which the sex object is valued as something more than a sexy body. Nevertheless, preliminary analyses such as Bartky's (and Eames' as well) are important because they allow us to identify what is needed for a more complete and accurate account of sex objectification.

3. SEX OBJECTS AS HARMED OBJECTS

It has been argued in this book that the "objectification" in sex objectification is in fact dehumanization, the *prima facie* inappropriate treatment of a person as a thing, body, part of body, or animal. Some
philosophers, however, see the "sex" in sex objectification as the key to
explaining the dehumanization that seems implicit in this phenomenon. Robert Baker and Ann Garry note,[30] as this book has done, that
when women complain about being regarded as sex objects, ". . . the
charge is that in our society men treat women as sex objects rather
than as persons," that men automatically conceive of women who sexually stimulate them ". . . as something less than human."[31] And
Garry claims that ". . . on the feminist view, all women really are full-
fledged people, it is just that some are treated as sex objects and perhaps think of themselves as sex objects."[32] Furthermore, both authors
support Eames' view that the complaints against sex objectification
are not merely complaints about being the focus or aim of another's
sexual desire. Baker notes the misconception in thinking that not
wanting to be regarded as a sex object means no more than not wanting to be regarded as "someone to have sex with," agreeing that such a
desire smacks of a puritanism that those who complain about such regard do not endorse.[33] And Garry suggests that although some people
may believe that sex is dirty, and so define two classes of women, good
and bad (pedestal and gutter, pure and defiled), those women who are
actively opposed to treating women as sex objects reject such
assumptions.[34]

However, both authors claim, unlike this book, that what charac-
terizes sex objectification, and explains the complaints women have
against it, is the male (and female) conceptual association of sex with
harm.[35] On this view, the female role in sexual intercourse is conceived of as the role of the passive victim of injurious sexual assault.
The man as sexual subordinator is the harmer, the woman as sexual
subordinate the harmed. Both authors argue that the evidence for the
conceptual connection between sex and harm lies in the language we
use to talk about sexual intercourse. Garry reviews Baker's conceptual
analysis of the terms "fuck" and "screw": ". . . in their traditional use,
'fuck' and 'screw' have taken a male subject, a female object, and have
had at least two meanings: harm and sexual intercourse."[36] The con-

notations of harm, according to both authors, are evident in such expressions as "fuck you," "screw you," or "up yours." In Baker's words, ". . . one of the strongest ways of telling someone that you wish to harm him [sic] is to tell him to assume the female sexual role relative to you."[37] To regard a woman as a sex object is to regard that woman as a harmed object. And such a conception, according to Baker, ". . . is antithetical to the conception of women as human beings — as persons rather than objects."[38] The woman as sex object is dehumanized, because the woman as *sex* object is a *harmed* object.

There are two important features to notice about this analysis. First, it is an analysis about how women are conceived of in sexual intercourse, based on how we talk about the male and female roles in sexual intercourse. Thus, it would be a mistake to think that either Baker or Garry consider it a necessary feature of sex objectification that the male sex objectifier actually harm his object. That is, the conceptual connection we are after is not of the form "whenever A has sex with B, A harms B." The cases of sex objectification outlined in Chapter I can elucidate this point. For example, the free spirit was not portrayed as upset because the construction workers had actually physically abused her, but because they had embarrassed and humiliated her. Even the assistant manager may have been afraid she might be fired if she did not comply with her president's request, but she did not regard his office (nor did he) as the arena for a sexual assault. And the unhappy wife was clearly not worried about any physical brutality her drunken husband might visit upon her. Furthermore, while the free spirit, unhappy wife, and assistant manager were all emotionally (albeit not physically) abused by their self-appointed sex partners, the case of the silent starer suggests that even this psychological component may be absent. So too, if the attitudes behind such a stare never find their way into practice, as small a possibility as this may be, then any economic, political, or other oppression as a direct consequence of such attitudes (the "harm" in this case) will never be actualized. One might think that the feelingless object would be the more liable to abuse by persons than something with sensations those persons can and should take into proper account in their treatment of it. But, as we suggested in Chapter II, objects may be treated with special care, even affection, as well as abuse. Furthermore, according to Baker and Garry, the harm is a way to explain or imply the dehumanization, and not the other way around. An examination of whether or not this implication is plausible follows below. For now, we can simply recognize, along with Baker and Garry, that to claim that a conceptual connection exists between sex and harm one need not also claim that the focus of one's sexual desire be actually harmed.

If we must not mistake the objectifier's concept of harm implicit in his concept of sex for harmful or abusive action, so too we must not regard the conceptual connection between sex and harm as a necessarily conscious one. The second feature to point out in Baker and Garry's analysis is that they are not claiming anything about individual men's and women's conscious conceptions about sex and its relationship to harm. Thus, their thesis is not "when A has sex with B, A consciously intends to harm B." This is not denying that there are men who actively seek out someone with whom they can have sexual intercourse, with the express purpose of using sex as a tool to harm that person. And there are those whose fantasies about sexual intercourse with others are conspicuously linked to fantasies of harming those persons or being harmed. But this is not to suggest that such conscious associations of sex with harm are necessary to an explanation of sex objectification. Still, they would argue, language does reflect attitudes, if only the prevailing attitudes of a particular society, and not every individual member of it. Therefore, the language we use to talk about sex can be used to illustrate that the way we think about sex, consciously or unconsciously, is in some way bound up in the idea that men harm those women with whom they have sex. Furthermore, those whom men harm in this way are *dehumanized*. Garry states that ". . . because in our culture we connect sex with harm that men do to women and think of the female role in sex as that of harmed object, we can see that to treat a woman as a sex object is automatically to treat her as *less than fully human*."[39] And Baker states that an important "*antihumanism* [is] implicit in the male concept of sex. . ."[40] (my emphasis).

Although theories in the psychoanalytic literature are mixed as to the specific structure of the relationships between sex and harm that exist in the unconscious, there is relative agreement among authors that desires that spring from the same libidinal source may be satisfied by many of the same stimuli.[41] Sexual desire and the desire to harm (an aggressive desire) are two such libidinal, or instinctual desires. Thus, there is no reason to deny that there may be an important psychic connection that exists in all of us, at various unconscious levels, between sex and harm. But for this connection to bear significantly on the complaint that the woman as sex object is treated as an object and not a person (in ways she should be treated as a person), then the sex/harmed object must also be a dehumanized object. Again, some of the psychoanalytic literature appears to speak to this point. Garry cites Robert J. Stoller's claim that sexual excitement is linked with a desire to harm another person, where ". . . the key process of sexual excitement can be seen as dehumanization (fetishization) in fantasy of the desired person."[42]

However, such psychic connections do not do the work Baker and Garry seem to have in mind. When Baker says dehumanization is "*implicit* in the male *concept* of sex" (my emphasis) or when Garry says to treat a woman as a sex/harmed object is "automatically" to treat her as less than fully human, the connection between sex and dehumanization which they affirm is a logical connection between propositions about sex and propositions about dehumanization, not some contingent psychological connection between our unconscious desires for sex and our unconscious wishes to dehumanize the object of these desires. Moreover, how would one argue against the claim that "A has sex with B" logically implies "A unconsciously harms B" or that "A unconsciously (or consciously) harms B" logically implies "A unconsciously dehumanizes B," when we can never discover exactly what our unconscious is up to? We often do actually harm persons without violating their rights as moral equals, as when we punish persons "for their own good" or harm persons by accident or mistake. So there is no necessary connection between the propositions "A harms B" and "A dehumanizes B." Then what is the link that Baker and Garry see between harm in sex and dehumanization?

Suppose we assume that what Baker and Garry mean by dehumanization is what I mean by dehumanization, viz. treating persons as objects but not also as moral equals. Both authors correctly regard the feminist slogan "Women ought not be treated as sex objects" as an injunction against treating women as objects of sexual desire in a *prima facie* inappropriate way, in a way which makes them out to be things, bodies, or animals but not also persons with certain human rights to well-being and freedom. Given they are convinced that in our culture we associate the act of sex with harming the female sex partner (consciously or unconsciously), they might then say that any man who makes such associations will not view his female sex partner as one who has a right against such harm. One's sex partner would be considered appropriately, or not inappropriately, harmed in sex. In such a case, the sex partner, by implication, is dehumanized in so far as she is not considered deserving of the level of well-being that her sex partner enjoys. She is not considered a moral equal in sex, but rather a sex *object*.

I shall assume that this is the most plausible (or one of the most plausible) interpretations of Baker's and Garry's thesis without either setting up a straw man or straying from the spirit of their analysis. However, one problem is that it is extremely difficult to discern what the basis is for the connection they claim exists between sex and dehumanization. Indeed, it is necessary to draw on the analysis of sex objectification in Chapter I of this book to clarify what they might mean by the term "dehumanization." Thus, this discussion may be accused of misrepresenting their work.[43] But if the above outline is something like what they have in mind, then there are several problems with it and with related notions in both Baker's and Garry's articles.

First, if we accept Baker's and Garry's analysis, it seems we are committed to the view that all sexual relations are conceived, at least on an unconscious level, as fundamentally dehumanizing. This runs contrary to the intuition of many (Baker and Garry included) that there is an important conceptual distinction to be made between treating a woman as sexy and treating her as a sex object. Because Baker and Garry use the "sex" in sex object to capture the complaint of dehumanization, they have no way of distinguishing, on a conceptual level, satisfied female sex partners from dissatisfied female sex objects. If language does reflect attitudes, and we do speak of treating a woman as sexy as opposed to treating her as an object, then such language would suggest we should find room in our conceptual scheme for non-objectifying sex.

Second, Baker suggests that the best, and by implication the most illuminating way to read the feminist slogan "Do not treat women as sex objects" is to read it solely as a rejection of the conception of the female role in sex as that of harmed object. In explanation of the slogan, he writes, "Our present conception of sexuality is such that to be a man is to be a person capable of brutalizing women . . . Such a conception . . . is clearly inimical to the best interests of women. It is only natural for women to reject such a sexual role . . . "[44] The analysis of sex objectification presented in Chapters I and II of this book suggests that women typically not only want to reject a role that places them in the position of one "brutalized" or physically abused, but any sexual role in which they are treated as the right and proper sexual subordinates of men. Baker's implication that the sex object is conceived of as the physically harmed object here only confuses the issue; he would certainly agree that men could virtually stop conceiving of women as passive victims of physical assault, but continue to cause them undue psychological distress, e.g. by humiliating them in the ways suggested in Chapter II, or continue to impose their own sexual preferences and stereotypes on women in a way that violates their rights to live autonomous lives. The concept of harm that Baker and Garry use simply covers too much ground to be left unanalyzed, or to be left synonymous with "brutalize."

Furthermore, Baker states that the slogan "Do not treat women as sex objects" cannot possibly mean "Do not treat women *exclusively* as sex partners" since as companions, servants, mothers, and so on, women are regarded by everyone as more than just sex partners. Thus, according to Baker, it is a slogan that everyone can agree with (including the male chauvinist) without changing her or his attitudes or practices in any way.[45] However, Baker fails to allow for the context in which sex objectification occurs. In certain contexts, for example, in the executive suite or in intellectual circles, some men do think of women, or some particular woman, exclusively as sex objects.[46] Moroever, a woman treated as a sex object in such contexts is not simply treated as a desirable sexual being in socially inappropriate circumstances. This would hardly explain the loss of privacy and self-respect that she typically feels, nor would it explain the domination and control that are common features of dehumanizing personal relationships. The sex objectifier in the boardroom is a dehumanizer in that context, not a conscientious potential lover who has made a relatively unobjectionable social *faux pas*. But only a reading of sex object as a sex "thing" and in particular, as "sexual subordinate," and not as "sex partner" can clearly separate these facts. A sex object is harmed in so far as she is degraded from status of moral equal to moral subordinate by her objectifier. However, she relatively seldom complains of being brutalized by her objectifier or even that her objectifier thinks of her as one to be brutalized; nor does she necessarily speak of sex only in dehumanizing terms.

Furthermore, it is unclear exactly why it is that conceiving of women as harmed in sex dehumanizes them. As mentioned above, there is no logical connection between the two; and there are numerous cases of treating persons as objects, as noted in Chapter I, that seem completely unobjectionable. Moreover, although there is a long philosophical tradition behind the claim that all persons ought to be respected as persons, or, in the terms used in this book, as moral equals, there is much dispute over what is wrong with the failure to accord persons this respect. Does it have consequences that wrong the dehumanized? Or is it wrong in itself, so that one may object even if the consequences are equitable? The strength of the characterization presented in this book is that it analyzes the implications of treating someone as the kind of thing whose rights to well-being and freedom are considered either more restricted or non-existent when compared to those of persons. The characterization of sex objectification presented can explain the complaints that the sex object makes in the context in which the dehumanization occurs by making a clear distinction between those cases in which it is appropriate for persons to be treated as objects and those cases in which it is not. A clear account of dehumanization is presented in order to explain why someone might think sex objectification is demeaning or degrading. In addition, the possibility is left open that someone might regard sex objectification as objectionable in some instances and relatively unobjectionable in others.

Each alternative characterization of sex objectification examined above makes a significant contribution to understanding the dilemma faced by the sex object. Eames asks us to make the important distinction between sex "thing" and sexual "objective;" and she locates the complaint of the sex object squarely on the issue of treating persons as objects. Bartky notices how much women are sexualized by our culture, even in situations where the context is inappropriate for initiating sexual encounters. Women are sexually objectified as a way of maintaining dominance and control over them; they are made to see themselves as men see them. Baker and Garry discuss the asymmetry between the way women are conceived in heterosexual sex and the way men are conceived. The female sex object is conceived of in our culture as one harmed in sex, whereas the male sex object is not. This asymmetry helps explain why women complain about being treated as sex objects, while men do not, and it reflects the kind of social double standard that encourages men to be the subordinators of women.

Chapters I and II of this book have sought to clarify further the meaning of and objections to treating a person as a sex object, as well as to describe some of the features of contemporary culture that tend to reinforce, even applaud, women's sex objectification by men. If we accept the critical analysis of sex objectification offered thus far, we can now ask: is the consent which a women in contemporary Western society gives to her own sex objectification morally justified?

NOTES

1 *See Journal of Thought* 11, No. 2 (April, 1976), pp. 140–143.

2 Eames, *op. cit.*, p. 142.

3 *Ibid.*, p. 143.

4 *Ibid.*

5 *Ibid.*, p. 142.

6 However, not all "uses" of persons are uses that treat persons as objects, or that are objectionable. This point was made at the end of Chapter I, section 6. Persons are used to run errands, and persons are used to hold ladders while others fix the roof. And directors have been known to use up to one thousand extras for one motion picture, all without moral or other censure. Moreover, when I selfishly get my own way by encouraging you to pursue your own goals or by inducing you to believe I am your friend, I may be using you in an objectionable way; but if I conceive of you as one with goals, friends, and so on, it seems inaccurate to say that I have treated you like an inanimate or non-human thing. In addition, in review of what was mentioned in Chapter I at the beginning of section 2, disregarding at least some of a person's desires is often done out of a concern for that person's welfare, as when I keep a young child out of the rain, despite her protests, because I know she will catch cold. Another example was the well-meaning concern for my friend's health, which motivates me to ignore her desires for a second helping of dessert. Even when I do disregard a person's interests in an objectionable manner, for example, by swiping a partner's pen just as she is about to use it, this hardly constitutes treating her as an inanimate thing. I may act as if she has no interests in the use of that pen, but not as if she has no interests at all. For example, compare swiping her pen to the act of picking her up bodily and flinging her across the room. In both cases I may "disregard her interests" (her interest in using her pen and in sitting in one corner of the room, respectively), but only the latter case entails treating her like a volleyball or bedspread, viz. as an inanimate thing.

7 See Judith Tormey, "Exploitation, Oppression, and Self-Sacrifice" in *Women and Philosophy*, ed. Carol C. Gould and Marx W. Wartofsky (New York: G. P. Putnam's Sons, 1976), pp. 206ff.

8 Tormey, *op. cit.*, p. 210.

9 Eames, *op. cit.*, p. 142.

10 For more on this argument as it concerns pornography, *see* Ann Garry, "Pornography and Respect for Women" in *Philosophy and Women*, ed. Sharon Bishop and Marjorie Weinzweig (Belmont, California: Wadsworth Publishing Co., 1979), pp. 133ff. For the thesis that prostitution is a means for men to subordinate women unjustly, *see* Alison Jaggar, "Prostitution" in *Philosophy of Sex*, ed. Alan Soble (Totowa: New Jersey: Littlefield, Adams & Co., 1980), pp. 358ff.

11 Eames, *op. cit.*, p. 141.

12 *See* Sandra Lee Bartky, "On Psychological Oppression" in Bishop and Weinzweig, *op. cit.*, pp. 36–38.

13 Bartky, *op. cit.*, p. 36.

14 *Ibid.*, p. 37.

15 For this interpretation of "mere" in reference to treating persons merely as means, *see* Thomas E. Hill, Jr., "Humanity as an End of Itself," *Ethics* 91, No. 3 (October, 1980), p. 87.

16 *Ibid.*, pp. 36–38.

17 *Ibid.*, p. 37.

18 *Ibid.*, p. 36.

19 *See* her footnote 9, *Ibid.*, p. 37.

20 *See* Thomas Nagel, "Sexual Perversion" and Sara Ruddick, "Better Sex" in *Philosophy and Sex,* ed. Robert Baker and Frederick Elliston (Buffalo, New York: Prometheus Books, 1975), pp. 247–260; pp. 83–104.

21 *See* Jean-Paul Sartre, *Being and Nothingness,* trans. Hazel E. Barnes (New York: Washington Square Press, 1966), p. 507.

22 *See* Nagel, *op. cit.*, pp. 256ff.

23 For Sartre's discussion of the sadist, *see* Sartre, *op. cit.*, pp. 494ff.

24 Eames, *op. cit.*, p. 141.

25 Bartky, *op. cit.*, p. 37.

26 *Ibid.*

27 *Ibid.*

28 *Ibid.*

29 *See infra* Chapter I, section 6.

30 *See* Robert Baker, " 'Pricks' and 'Chicks': A Plea for Persons" in Baker and Elliston, *op. cit.*, pp. 45–64; *also see* Ann Garry, "Pornography and Respect for Women," *op. cit.*, pp. 128–139.

31 Baker, *op. cit.*, pp. 56–57.

32 Garry, *op. cit.*, p. 136.

33 Baker, *op. cit.*, p. 55.

34 Garry, *op. cit.*, pp. 135–136.

35 Baker, *op. cit.*, pp. 57–63; Garry, *op. cit.*, pp. 136–137.

36 Garry, *op. cit.*, p. 136.

37 Baker, *op. cit.*, p. 61.

38 *Ibid.*, p. 57.

39 Garry, *op. cit.*, p. 136.

40 Baker, *op. cit.*, p. 57.

41 For an interesting application of this claim to the realm of sexual excitement, *see* Robert J. Stoller, *Sexual Excitement: Dynamics of Erotic Life* (New York: Pantheon Books, 1979).

42 Garry, *op. cit.*, p. 136. The article from which this summary is taken is Stoller's "Sexual Excitement," *Archives of General Psychiatry* 33 (August, 1976), esp. p. 903.

43 For another author's attempt at unraveling this connection, *see* Stephanie Ross, "How Words Hurt: Attitude, Metaphor, and Oppression" in *Sexist Language,* ed. Mary Vetterling-Braggin (Totowa, New Jersey: Littlefield, Adams & Co., 1981), pp. 202ff.

44 Baker, *op. cit.*, p. 63.

45 *Ibid.*, p. 55.

46 *See* Michael Korda, *Male Chauvinism! How It Works* (New York: Ballantine Books, 1973), Chapter 4 for just such contexts.

chapter 4

Ethics and Social Change

This concluding chapter discusses whether or not a woman's consent to her own sex objectification in contemporary society is sufficient reason for thinking the objectification morally permissible. We intend to show how sex objectification as dehumanization can be used to understand the complaints women make about their status in domestic, economic, political and social spheres. Also, there are some practical suggestions to the sex objects of our original examples in Chapter I: what can (or should) a woman do, if anything, when treated as a sex object by a man? We will examine the variety of alternatives that feminists have cited to try to rid society of sex objectification on a broad scale, and propose that the concept of moral equality can in principle provide a model for an ideal in sex that can accommodate both those who wish to subordinate or be subordinated in sex and those who do not.

Nothing is said explicitly below about whether or not a man's consent to his own sex objectification is ever morally justified. The reason for this is that it was argued in the last section of Chapter II that men typically are not successfully treated as sex objects by other women in contemporary society. Their consent to such treatment is consenting to a kind of reinforcement of their dominant status in sex and in the society at large. Thus, their enjoyment of being treated as sex objects is an enjoyment of being treated as sexually virile, competent, indeed morally superior *persons*.

However, as we saw in Chapter II, men can be successfully treated as sex objects by women (and other men); and they can consent to their own successful sexual subordination. Given that treating persons as less than moral equals in sex is *prima facie* wrong, then men's successful sex objectification by others or by themselves will be *prima facie* wrong. And if we could show that a man's consent to his successful sex objectification did create the sort of moral climate that encouraged the sex objectification of those who do not wish it, then such consent would have to be re-evaluated in light of those effects. Similarly, if self-interest does not provide adequate justification for a woman's consent to her successful sex objectification, neither will it provide adequate justification for a man. And if enough men do not wish to be treated successfully as sex objects, then considerations of general utility must include their happiness as well. Thus, the same methods of deriving any conclusions concerning the morality of consenting to women's successful sex objectification, if not the same conclusions, can be applied *mutatis mutandis* to the case of men. We must simply remember that our society's sexual ideology does not stereotype men as the sex objects of women, so that men's successful sex objectification will be relatively less frequent than that of women, and any consent that men give to their successful sex objectification will not reinforce a sexual stereotype of them as the sexual subordinates of women.

1. THE MORAL PERMISSIBILITY OF TREATING ONESELF AS A SEX OBJECT FOR OTHERS

Let us review the reasons a woman might give for treating herself as a sex object for others offered earlier in Chapter II. One reason she might give is that she does not think the treatment she permits is actually in violation of her rights to well-being and freedom or that it reflects a kind of inappropriate attitude toward what rights she is entitled to. She is someone who, on my characterization, does not consider herself to be treated as a true sex *object* or sexual *subordinate* by men at all.

A second reason she might give for treating herself as a sex object for others is that, while she finds it dehumanizing with respect to at least some of her rights to well-being and freedom, she believes the temporary waiver or overriding of such rights is justified by other sorts of benefits which she believes her sex objectification will bring her. Such benefits may be of an altruistic nature, such as when she raises money stripping to support her family, or they may be benefits which she feels she deserves, but that will be denied her unless she consents to her own sex objectification by others. This is the situation of the assistant manager and of many women in contemporary society. However, the consent of this second type, which is of primary concern for the following discussion, is not consent for moral reasons or other-regarding prudential reasons, or consent under duress, but consent due to self-interest. This is the woman who treats herself as a sex object for others because of the social status, fame, or fortune it will bring her, and who does not feel the kind of peer pressure some women feel that she must act this way or have no social status at all. She simply feels that her dehumanization is a small price to pay for the kinds of benefits she can reap from it. Television and movie actresses known for their roles in "Tits and Ass" subjects and glorified for same by the writers of film tabloids are typical examples.

The third case involves the woman who allows other men to treat her as a sex object because she is ignorant of or misunderstands what her rights to well-being and freedom are. Such a person is like the submissive wife who is convinced that her proper role is that of subordinate to her husband both in and out of bed. She is not simply trading what she believes are her moral rights for the benefits of economic and social security; she does not see herself as having such rights to trade. She may be contented with her lot or not; but she can be said to be either ignorant of or misunderstand the rights to well-being and freedom in her sexual relations that, as a moral equal, she in fact has.

A. Consent Due to Ignorance or a Misunderstanding of One's Moral Rights

We can consider this last case first. If the sex object is not content with her situation, the problem is relatively straightforward. Since her reasons for consenting to her sex objectification were that she did not think she had a right to anything better, once she is enlightened as to the moral rights she in fact has, we can expect that she will no longer willingly consent to her sex objectification. She was dissatisfied with her lot, but assumed there was no better treatment she could claim from others. Once she is convinced she has a right to be treated as a moral equal, we should expect that she will exercise those rights unless otherwise constrained from doing so. As noted in Chapter II, she may be thought partially to blame for her own situation if she has simply acted in blind acceptance of her culture's sexual ideology. Yet her consent is understandable in virtue of the kind of indoctrination that exists in much of that ideology and forgivable in light of her unwillingness to consent in the future.

The woman who without resignation willingly accepts her role as sex object for men is another story. She may not be so easily convinced that she actually has certain rights to well-being and freedom that are being overridden by men, or that her position is one that she would do better to avoid. The submissive wife described in Chapter II thought it was a woman's rightful place to serve her husband, and that, while she was not the mental or physical inferior of her husband, it was clear that his needs came first in their relationship; she may even be convinced that he could not achieve the kind of success in his professional life that he has without her constant deference and support of his pursuits. Compare Thomas E. Hill Jr.'s "deferential wife" in his discussion of servility and self-respect: ". . . she buys the clothes *he* prefers, invites the guest *he* wants to entertain, and makes love whenever *he* is in the mood . . . she tends not to form her own interests, values and ideals; and when she does, she counts them as less important than her husband's . . . [but] no one is trampling on her rights, she says; for she is quite glad, and proud, to serve her husband as she does."[1]

Suppose such a woman, as Professor Hill suggests, has simply failed to understand and acknowledge her own moral rights.[2] Since one's rights to well-being and freedom were based on the claim that without them, persons would lead more impoverished or less fulfilling lives than they might otherwise, one might try to enlighten such a person as to what her true rights are. One might explain to her that she acts and thinks the way she does in response to a kind of subtle social indoctrination of women; she has been raised in a culture that expects her to look at her social role in the way she does and approves of her behavior only when she meets those expectations.[3] However, she must not think that she has no other alternative life-choices, nor that it is her *duty* to fulfill her role as nurturer and caretaker for her husband's needs, sexual and otherwise. Perhaps she is not aware of the sorts of activities she could be pursuing and how much more fulfilling her own life could be, if she were free of the subordinating influence of her husband.

However, such a woman might come around to accepting the fact that she is deserving of the same moral rights as her husband yet nevertheless continue to allow him to treat her as a sex object. She may feel she owes him at least this much after years of his financial support. Or she may simply re-emphasize that she can be happy only when her husband is happy, or that it is too much trouble and there is too little tangible gain in trying to get him to change his attitudes. Or perhaps she simply refuses to believe that women have the same kinds of rights as men. It would seem that, unless we want to place the restriction on her that she *cannot,* without moral censure, waive her rights to well-being and freedom, then she is morally justified in continuing to act the way she does. For she is essentially saying that her own life would be less fulfilling or a more unhappy one if she were to act differently than she does, and these at least sound like the same sorts of grounds we used to justify the rights in the first instance.

However, the grounds for moral equality stipulated in Chapter II are such that *each* and *every* person be free from a certain minimum of physical and psychological distress, and that we be free to move about and express ourselves as we wish. If the wife's consent succeeds in making her life a happy one, but at the same time succeeds in making others' lives miserable, her consent would not be justified on the grounds of moral equality specified above. Suppose, for example, it were true that her actions only reinforce in her husband's mind an image of women as the proper sexual subordinates of men so that he treats other women who do not think like his wife in the same way he treats her, or so that he advocates his position toward women to other men. Her consent would thus encourage her husband and other men to violate the rights to well-being and freedom that other women enjoy in their sexual relations. Perhaps her informed consent does not create an opportunity for her husband to do anything wrong to her, but her consent can create a climate of legitimacy for others' rights to be violated.

Furthermore, women who do complain about their sex objectification by men do not seem to be able to create a climate equally favorable to their own views; thus the submissive wife cannot say that the actions of those who complain about their sex objectification violate her right to live the life she has chosen by engendering expectations in others that she does not wish to meet. The prevailing sexual ideology reinforces her way of thinking, not theirs. Even if pockets of protest became so strong that the submissive wife begins to feel pressured by other women to conform to their point of view, such a position would constitute a kind of moral stand-off, with climates equally conducive to either view. Such a social milieu hardly provides concrete evidence that consent is justified *over* the complaints of those who do not agree. A person's rights to well-being and freedom are justified not merely on the value of *some* persons' experiences, but on those of all persons. And while this does not demand that we take all persons' situations into account before deciding what to do (indeed, this would be practically impossible), it does demand that we consider how other persons may be immediately affected. Thus, the wife who treats herself as a sex object for her husband must take into account how her actions will affect at least some of those persons with whom she and her husband will come into social contact before she can morally justify her actions. We have given some reason for thinking that instantiating the prevailing sexual ideology only reinforces the *status quo,* and that for many women the *status quo* precludes their living a self-determined life, or a life of moral equality with men. Therefore, while such treatment may be legitimate in social isolation, it looks much less legitimate from within the prevailing sexual ideology of contemporary society.

B. Consent Due to Considerations of Self-Interest

Given the above considerations, the woman who sees her sex objectification as dehumanizing but is willing to waive some of her moral rights in the name of self-interest is on even shakier ground than the submissive wife. For while the wife has in mind the happiness of at least one other person, her husband, when she consents to her objectification by him, the sex objects in this category think only of themselves. As we mentioned above, while the grounds of moral equality take stock of what persons value, they are based on the interests of all persons equally, not just on the interests of a few. Also, our working hypothesis is that the principle stating that all persons ought to be treated as moral equals is the sort of principle the rights under which cannot be legitimately waived by free and informed consent alone. Thus, philosophers have argued that any considerations that might justify waiving or overriding *prima facie* rights such as those under consideration must be moral considerations[4] or considerations of justice,[5] not merely prudential or self-interested ones. Therefore, the sex object will not be able to justify consenting to that which is *prima facie* wrong, simply because she likes the attention or the money or the fancy job. Furthermore, we can argue that her consent legitimizes a climate for the violation of the rights of other women in their sexual relations in the same way we argued above in the case of the submissive wife. If she is convinced that she creates no such climate or claims that she should not be held responsible for what others do, we can argue that since she does not live in social isolation, she can be held at least partially accountable for how her actions affect those around her. And since her actions only tend to reinforce the *status quo,* her actions can only tend to reinforce the very climate which other women find objectionable, and for which they have no other alternative.

However, the fact that such women may be held at least partially accountable for their choice of sex objectification should not be interpreted as suggesting that they are the only persons to be held morally responsible. While women may perpetuate and even help create the expectations in the minds of both women and men that women are primarily the sexual subordinates of men, men create and maintain those expectations as well. In fact, an argument can be made that if men are regarded as the paradigmatically active subjects in the world, defining women (the passive objects of their inquiry) as their sexual subordinates, then it is not the inactive thing who should be called into account but the active subject whose responsibility it is for defining women as sex objects.[6] Yet such an argument seems only to reinforce the view that women are passive objects incapable of informed moral decision. Women can and should be held at least partially responsible for any actions they perform or any attitudes they entertain that perpetuate an unfair social situation of which they, living in a society of heightened feminist consciousness, have every reason to be aware. This is not to lay the blame for sex objectification on their shoulders, but to argue that women can be not only victims of sex objectification, but also the perhaps unwitting victimizers as well. The question raised here is not one of ideals, viz. how do we want men to treat women in the ideal society? It is one of social realities: given men treat women as sex objects, and given we do not live in social isolation but in a world where social expectations can be reinforced simply by continuing to think and act in the ways expected, are women morally justified in consenting to their own (avowedly self-interested) sex objectification by others? The claim here is that, given the social realities, women are not so justified, at least not as conclusively as if their actions affected no one but themselves.

Arguments from general utility which the self-interested sex object might address are also inconclusive. Suppose she asserts that since she finds pleasure in her sex objectification, and that other men do as well, she ought, on utilitarian grounds, to be able to continue. On the other hand, there are arguably as many women who do not enjoy being treated as sex objects, and as many men who would like to stop being subtly but successfully pressured by many of their peers to continue to subordinate women sexually. Furthermore, if by her consent the sex object reinforces the expectation in the minds of those men with whom she comes in contact that other women will act similarly, then, even if we stipulate that it is men who initially create those expectations, she may be fostering more unhappiness than happiness for non-consenting women by what she does. In any event, she cannot use the pleasure that certain others derive from what she does to justify conclusively what she does.

And finally, we can ask whether a woman's sex objectification is or is not, in fact, in her long-term self-interest. For although present satisfaction in the form of attention from other men or easy money may be forthcoming, the long-term benefits of such consent dwindle by comparison. What plans does such a woman have for her future when her face wrinkles and her breasts sag? The attention that she succeeds in getting at present is attention that will lag with age. Even if her posing for *Playboy* is a temporary sideline or hobby alongside a relatively lucrative professional career, she may not fully understand the portrait she projects in her poses. While we can point a moral finger at those men who would create or buy into a sexual ideology that advocates that women are the proper subordinates of men, such an ideology is also swallowed whole by the woman who has effectively stated by her *Playboy* posture that she is willing to be the sexual "bunny" or "pet" of the public at large. It is a sexual ideology that demeans women and regards them as being less serious about themselves and generally less valuable than men. The real problem certainly lies in the creation of such an ideology in the first place. But, given that its creation is objectionable, its unwarranted perpetuation is so as well. Moreover, those women who consent to be treated as the sex objects of their boyfriends or husbands, as well as those stripping and posing for *Play-*

boy, may not enjoy being treated as sex objects in other areas of their lives. The stripper may not accept the sexual subordination of her husband nor the *Playboy* bunny an offer of sex in exchange for a promotion. Yet what they consent to only reinforces a general view of women as the proper sex objects of men. If they do not wish to be sex objects under some conditions, they would do well to avoid consenting to being sex objects under any conditions. Again, the key factor to bear in mind is that such consent occurs within a social milieu whose sexual ideology develops much of its strength from the obedience to it of those who live in that milieu. And the stronger the sexual ideology, the more its strength will translate into intimidation and psychological domination for those who would care to act or think differently than the ideology dictates.

C. Consent Due to the Failure to See Sex Objectification as Dehumanization

By far the most common reason that might be given for consenting to what appears to be one's sex objectification by others comes from those women who see nothing wrong with their treatment at all. They do not consider their rights to well being and freedom violated in their sexual relations with men nor do they consider inappropriate the sexual attitudes that men have for them. They like being considered sexy; and they find a real kind of self-esteem in the knowledge that men consider them so. Anyone who says they are not free to express themselves in sex simply misunderstands what they want out of their sexual relationships.

One response to be made to such women is that while they may feel free from male sexual oppression, they nevertheless perpetuate an oppressive sexual climate for women by wearing the symbols associated with the unjust subordination of women by other men. Such women advertise submission in the way they think, act, or dress, even if they do not themselves feel oppressed, or are lucky enough to meet only those men who treat them as moral equals. A woman in this category may counter that it is the oppressors of women who perpetuate the stereotype of woman as sex object and not herself, so it is unfair to condemn her activities when the real problem lies outside herself. The rejoinder advocated here is that since men (and many women) do conceive of women as the proper sex objects of men, one cannot ignore what one's own actions may communicate to those conceivers nor what consequences one's actions within that conceptual community will have for others. It is the sexually oppressive social climate in which her actions take place that commits her to doing more than just noticing that men treat women as sex objects and then going about her business. Her own personal life is necessarily one with political ramifications whether she rejects those ramifications or not.

Another response such women might make to the claim that they unfairly reinforce an oppressive sexual climate for other women is that because of the particular men with whom they socialize, they feel convinced that they are not in fact being regarded as less than moral equals by such men; therefore, they see nothing dehumanizing about taking special pride and care in being sexually attractive for them. It is in keeping with our characterization of sex objectification to say that *if* such women can show that they are not in fact being regarded as less than the moral equals of the men for whom they take special pride in being sexually attractive, then they are right to see nothing wrong with their treatment as I have described it. The contention of this book, however, has been that sex is an extremely effective vehicle for the dehumanization of women in contemporary society. It can be used to exploit women, to brutalize women, to threaten women, to humiliate women, to make them feel socially inferior or just plain dirty. Moreover, the prevailing sexual ideology engenders in men the false belief that they are the solely competent, the properly dominant, the morally superior partner in their sexual relationships. Thus, even when a woman responds with a smile instead of humiliation to men such as our construction workers, or contentedly allows her sexist husband to make love whenever he is in the mood, or acquiesces in secret satisfaction to the offer of sex in exchange for a promotion from an attractive albeit manipulative boss, she is nevertheless being regarded as the proper sexual subordinate of those men when she is in fact their moral equal. The point is that whether or not she feels dehumanized, this is no reason to think that, especially in a culture which reinforces the sex objectification of women, she is not being dehumanized in fact.[7] The fact that any women would choose to subordinate their sexual interests to men because they would not even think of doing otherwise, is simply a sign of the power of a sexual ideology which is unconsciously adopted and unconsciously approved of.[8] There is no reason to think that the women who do not feel unfairly subordinated

in sex are not in fact being subordinated by men who have adopted the
sexual attitudes that their ideology dictates. Until a woman's sexuality in our culture becomes a feature of her personality which makes
her as much a competent, independent person among her peers as it
does men, women ought to be skeptical that there is nothing wrong
with being valued solely or primarily as a sexual attraction to men.

2. THE MORAL PERMISSIBILITY OF TREATING ONESELF AS A SEX OBJECT FOR ONESELF

We have suggested that if the consenting sex object could justify her
consent on the same kinds of grounds upon which the moral equality
of persons is justified, then her consent would be unobjectionable.
That is, the woman who treats herself as a sex object must somehow
show that her life would be more impoverished without such treatment and that such treatment does not interfere with the pursuit of
others' competing rights. Therefore, simply to say that the actions of
the sex-objectifying masturbator dehumanize her and are therefore
wrong is too facile, given the rules on exceptions given above. We
must first ask why she might masturbate in this way in order to see if
her reasons fit the criteria for justification mentioned.

These reasons fall into the same general categories as those in the
previous section. This is true in virtue of the fact that both kinds of
treatment imply waiving one's rights to well-being and freedom,
thereby allowing others to treat one as less than a moral equal. So, for
example, a woman may masturbate in the way she does because she
does not believe that either her behavior or her attitudes toward herself dehumanize her. She may assert that while it appears that she regards herself as worthy only of humiliation, she does not believe this
herself. Masturbating on the command of another is, among other
things, the way she likes sex. She does not waive any of her rights to
moral equality; therefore she cannot be accused of creating a climate
of legitimacy for others to treat persons as less than moral equals. If
others regard her actions as dehumanizing, that is their mistake.

The problem with this line of argument is that it denies the fact that
what appears to women as perfectly legitimate sex nevertheless occurs
within a prevailing sexual climate in which the oppression of women

is regarded as inevitable, if not best, and where masturbation is still regarded by many as necessarily dehumanizing. Ideally, we want to change those attitudes, but given their entrenchment, one's actions must be judged within the larger context. A privacy argument works only if one does in fact keep one's masturbation to oneself; but even here, we must ask that if a woman is socialized under the sexual double standard discussed in Chapter II, how much of her behavior is a product of that oppression and how much of it is a product of a freer atmosphere? Such questions remain open, but the point is to notice that because women have been taught (even rewarded) for seeing themselves as less than moral equals often without their awareness, the burden falls on those who believe their actions do not perpetuate that oppression to show this.

Those who masturbate in a dehumanizing fashion because they do not believe they deserve any better can be apprised of the moral equality they do deserve. But what of those who do so, acknowledging it is dehumanizing, but who wish to continue because they like that kind of sex? They would say they may be waiving their rights to well-being and freedom by humiliating themselves in public, but this turns them on. It would appear that such a woman's behavior would then be justified on the grounds that her sex life would be seriously impoverished without this. But again, the response focuses on the social climate within which the dehumanizing masturbation takes place. Given the already pervasive view that women deserve to be humiliated sexually, any actions by those women who appear to choose to humiliate themselves can only reinforce that view. Such reinforcement will have a negative impact on other women who do not so choose by creating real and subtle pressures on them to endure being the sex objects of others, pressures in the form of the restrictive social expectations listed in Chapter II. We can even question, as above, how much of the choice a woman says she makes to contribute to her own dehumanization is in fact a product of an indoctrination of her, aimed at convincing her she deserves no more. If she were living in social isolation, or in a climate with a different prevailing sexual ideology, her actions might be shown to have no adverse effects on others. But if she does publicly acknowledge, much less praise, her dehumanizing sexual habits, this must be judged for its ability to reinforce a sexual climate notorious for its subtle indoctrination to the *status quo* of patriarchy.

3. WOMEN: THE DEHUMANIZED SEX

The main thesis of this book has been that women are systematically sexualized by men in a way that dehumanizes women and in a way to which men as a sex do not fall prey with the same frequency, indignity, or social consequence. But the feminist cry for sex equality is not only a cry for equality in sexual relations,[9] but a plea for moral equality in other social relations as well. Women are systematically dehumanized in the domestic sphere, the economic, and the political spheres as well. And women are dehumanized psychologically so that they believe that their position as the social subordinates of men is either necessary, inevitable, deserved or, if the psychologizing is complete, right and best. Sex objectification only brings into graphic relief a woman's social status as subordinated, other-defined object for man the defining subject. Given these observations, the preceding analysis of sex objectification as a kind of dehumanization can serve as a means of understanding the nature and objections to women's oppression on a broad scale.

First, in spite of the partial breakdown of the male professional world by working women, women are domesticated by contemporary culture in a way which dehumanizes them. They are stereotyped first and foremost as persons whose primary responsibility is to marry a financially sustaining man and bear and raise his children. Only recently, *Newsweek* began its description of Nobel Laureate Barbara McClintock, not with a list of her achievements in the study of genetics, but with the observation that, as the "Greta Garbo of genetics" at 81, "she has never married, always preferring to be alone,"[10] as if she had shirked her primary responsibility as wife and mother in order to pursue a life in a "man's world." This kind of stereotyping is objectionable because it is in violation of a woman's right to live an autonomous life, free not of all role expectations, but of those that would intimidate or indoctrinate her into being other than she might choose to be in the absence of those expectations. Furthermore, the role itself is a dehumanizing one. A woman is not only raised in the culture to regard herself as the primary caretaker of a husband and children (whatever else she does), but she is not paid for her labor and so regarded primarily as an unpaid, even though not unskilled, laborer. Thus she is exploited labor in a profit-taking economy yet at the same time devalued as a person who does not (really) "work." She remains the passive object to man's active subject. She is defined as the lesser in value of the two sexes in a society that gives her double messages by putting her on a motherhood pedestal that is itself on a lower plane than that of a man. Without easily accessible, affordable day care, she is too often unfairly restricted in her freedom of movement and expression by being restricted to caring for her home and children when she may not always be the willing or even desirable caretaker. Without readily accessible contraceptives in some areas or readily available abortion clinics, she may feel forced to accept her prescribed maternal role before she might wish. And if she does play that role and does not also try to secure a "real job," she remains dependent upon her husband, if she has one, or her family, or the state, for financial support.[11]

If a woman does work, the process of choosing her work as well as the nature of the work itself can be dehumanizing in a way it will not be for a man. Because of an entrenched "old boy network," from which so many opportunities for training as well as opportunities for skilled jobs are secured, many professionally-trained women who can afford day care and domestic help are still excluded from jobs for which they might otherwise be qualified. Such a male network often allows women into middle-management but no higher; it continues to compensate women financially far less than men in the same job category. And by confining the majority of working women to jobs with relatively low job status (clerk, secretary, elementary school teacher, nurse), women as a sex are redefined as the inferior sex. Men can benefit from the present division of labor by sex by taking advantage of those positions that would otherwise be held by women, and enjoying the freedom that comes with having someone else do one's more mundane chores.[12] One argument against the claim that affirmative action programs constitute unfair "reverse discrimination" is that such programs would neutralize this unfair advantage by removing the obstacles women face in training for and securing the jobs they qualify for; they do not seek to rectify an injustice with another injustice.[13]

Women are the dehumanized sex in party politics as well. There remain as of this writing only a handful of women in Congress and the Cabinet in comparison to their male counterparts. They are often given jobs that purportedly require a "feminine" touch, such as health or human services work. Because of their domestic subordination they often have little of their own money to spend on campaigning and advertising, and they tend to be criticized when they do gain political appointments with the claim that they shouldn't be doing a man's job anyway.[14]

In short, women as a sex are treated as less than the moral equals of men in more than just the sexual sphere; their sex objectification is simply paradigmatic of the kind of dehumanization they suffer in other social arenas. Women are referred to, thought about, and acted toward as the primary caretakers of home and hearth, whatever else they do, as nurturant and intuitive, but at the same time vain, hysterical, and so unfit for the rational, working world of men. While men may suffer the pressures of being "success objects"[15], they are not pegged inferior as a sex by their attempts to compete for social status and power, for scarce resources, or to secure self-respect or self-esteem. Even if we could show that women were only capable of doing certain sorts of things, of thinking certain sorts of ways, still it is a further question what value we are to place on those capabilities or what role we decide they should play in the good society. It remains to be shown that women are in any way the proper or rightful subordinates of men; if, however, such subordination has tangible real benefits for men and at least superficial benefits for many women, women will remain the dehumanized sex until such benefits are seen as burdens for those who garner them in the name of Man the Provider.[16]

4. ALTERNATIVES FOR SOCIAL CHANGE

If the sex objectification of women, indeed any person, is objectionable as characterized in these pages, what might be done to eradicate the problem? First, if one has been convinced that the sex objectification of women is innate to the species or somehow condoned by evolution, the problem is not one of eradication, but one of resignation by feminists and promotion by chauvinists. But there is no reason to think this true. Suggesting that homosexual men and women can take up the socio-sexual roles typically played by their opposite sex is to suggest that the sexual ideology from which sex objectification springs is a part of our particular cultural or social psychology and not inherent in the biology of men and women.[17] Or suppose we imagine a world in which the social, economic, and political institutions were both inherited through and in the hands of women and not men, and that matriarchy, not patriarchy, were the historically dominant political trend. That is, suppose we imagine the power structure and lines of inheritance for that power in contemporary society and in all previous societies completely in reverse. Part of the discussion in Chapter II explained how easy it was for men to use their power in socioeconomic institutions to coerce or intimidate women into being their subordinates in sex. And the section immediately preceding suggests that the dehumanizer in sex is the dehumanizer in many other areas of social life as well. Because of these and similar facts, it can be argued that in the societies described above, men would be treated as sex objects in much the same way women are treated as sex objects today. Their subordination in the socio-economic spheres would foster and reflect their subordination in sex. And many men would find certain kinds of sex demeaning to them as persons or as means of marking them as prostitutes or social outcasts. In general, men, and not women, would regard sex as an effective vehicle for their dehumunization. Yet the very fact that it is our socioeconomic and political institutions that seem to foster and reinforce the sex objectification of some persons and not others, no matter which sex is in power, suggests that the sex objectification of women in contemporary society is a social or political, and not a biological reality. Even those who would place female sex objectification squarely within the psychoanalytic tradition argue that we can bring about social change by restructuring the role of the parent in the infant's early life.[18] Thus it would seem that as difficult as any social change might be, it is not an impossibility due to some inherent biology in men and women.[19]

If we accept the possibility that sex objectification can be the subject of substantial social change, then the alternatives for implementing change fall into two broad categories, short-term solutions and long-term solutions. A list of possible short-term solutions provides immediate options for the woman who is victimized by sex objectification; these alternatives are her practical weapons for combatting the problem when and where it occurs. Some long-term solutions are also necessary if we are to cure more than the symptoms of the disease. Thus, we need an outline of the options feminists discuss in combatting the sex objectification of women on a broad scale.

A. *Short-Term Solutions for the Free Spirit, the Unhappy Wife, and the Assistant Manager*

A representative sampling of some of the immediate practical suggestions we can give to the victim of sex objectification can be offered by turning to our original three examples in Chapter I. What can the free spirit, the unhappy wife, and the assistant manager say or do, if anything, to keep their predicament from occurring again? In the case of the free spirit and unhappy wife, pretending not to notice seems only to prolong the problem or, at worst, to give tacit approval of it. The free spirit might reroute her walk home from school, but she might meet more sex objectifiers on that route; and (albeit understandably) she leaves the original problem unresolved for others. This may even be her favorite walk home or the shortest; she would be the one who changes in response to the intransigence of her objectifiers. The unhappy wife could seek divorce or other lovers to escape her husband's subordination in bed, but she may love him for other reasons or feel she might lose her children or her job if she seeks other sexual outlets. As in the case of the free spirit, this avenue would leave the problem unaddressed for any other victims of her husband's sex objectification, nor could she be assured that she would not find herself in the same predicament again. The assistant manager cannot pretend not to notice, since she is directly propositioned. She could resign, but this avenue, it was supposed, would only reinforce the sexist view that women could not get ahead in the business world without sex.

All three women might decide to make a negative comment to show their displeasure, such as "that's disgusting!" or "shut up!" or even "fuck off!" in order not to give even tacit approval to the behavior. But, as we have seen, this commonly reinforces the false belief that women do not like sex or do not want to be sexually attractive. It can also be dangerous; the free spirit does not know her objectifiers, many of whom may be motivated by her curt remarks to abuse her further. The unhappy wife may also be the object of some verbal abuse by her husband who may not understand her rejection of him. If her husband cannot tolerate her reaction, he may cease his objectifying behavior, but then he may still think of her as his sex object and come to resent her way of thinking without understanding it. The assistant manager might again be without a job for returning the insult she deems she has received; at the very least, she may simply not want to bring herself to the level to which he has tried to reduce her by reacting with a demeaning remark.

All three women might try the opposite reaction, viz. smiling graciously as if they had just received personal compliments, but problems arise here also. First, the problem may continue, and even become exacerbated, by such approval. In fact, a smile from the assistant manager might well be interpreted as an immediate "Yes!" to the president's proposition. Also, by not being true to their feelings, all three will harbor resentment toward their objectifiers which, seeking an outlet, may emerge in inappropriate or unwelcome contexts.

A more interesting alternative is direct confrontation, telling the sex objectifier that what he does is degrading to oneself and women generally, and as such, is morally objectionable. While such an alternative seeks to enlighten the sex objectifier concerning a problem of which he may be unaware—while the above alternatives do not—this solution is far from problem-free. First, the free spirit may be very unwilling to confront her objectifiers at all. This predicament was paradigmatic of what we called a woman's "rape mentality," a mentality unparalleled in men whose stereotype defines them as physically and psychologically aggressive. If the free spirit does not feel physically threatened, she may still feel that the lack of acquaintance presents too awkward a social situation in which to moralize, so that any such words would be laughed off or left unheard. The unhappy wife may be in a less threatening situation for confrontation, but her husband may remain just as uncomprehending of her feelings and as dubious of the propriety of any moralizing at that particular moment. The assistant manager faces a problem that combines features of the previous two: she may risk being fired for her reactions, or she may simply face total incomprehension ("She must be gay or frigid"). There is also the possibility that such men know exactly what they are doing and need no such enlightenment.

Then there is the ideal situation where the objectifier listens carefully to the response, and asks for further clarification and insight. The rather sorry fact is that this situation seldom occurs. One of the frustrations for women being treated as sex objects is that there is so little we can do *at that moment* to ease the humiliation, the anger, and the anxiety that accompanies the treatment. It simply *happens*. This suggests that the apparent attitudes of the man who seeks the sexual subordination of women are attitudes that are (1) deeply rooted in the sexual ideology from which he learns his sexual role, (2) unquestioningly accepted in many cases, and (3) those that are associated with real and tangible social benefits. (See section 3 above.) The alternatives listed above are unsatisfying for the most part, just because they attempt to solve a problem that is much broader in scope than a single isolated event. If sex objectification is definitive of a broader social oppression of women as has been suggested, then the social institutions that foster and perpetuate that oppression are the real culprits. Changes in such institutions are far from quick, short-term, or certain of success.

B. Long-Term Solutions

The question of long-term solutions to the problem of sex objectification is a problem of preventive maintenance: what can be done to keep women, or any persons, from being the unwilling or unwitting victims of sex objectification? Suppose we agree that sex objectification does treat the sex object as less than a moral equal; still, one may disagree as to the root cause or origins of that dehumanization and so disagree as to how to go about preventing it. The liberal feminist is one who is convinced that changing the status of women under the present law is the key to preventing sex objectification. According to this view, a woman is regarded as less than a moral equal because she is not regarded as equal to men under the law. If there were strict enough laws against sexual harassment and sex discrimination in housing, employment, education, health, and welfare, men would stop treating women in this objectionable fashion. To make sure that their words match their deeds, consciousness-raising groups for both women and men would provide a conducive atmosphere for moral enlightenment and insure the continued success of sex equality in public policy.[20]

While the Marxist feminist agrees that sex equality needs to be written into the law, she does not think such change is sufficient. The Marxist feminist believes that the struggle for sex equality is rooted in class struggle, or more specifically, rooted in the exploitative political economy of capitalism. Once the shackles of dehumanizing and alienating labor have been thrown off in favor of a socialist economy, men and women will work together in cooperation and harmony. Men will no longer treat women as sex objects to be owned, used, or abused at will, because they will no longer see their social status in terms of private property. Thus, women can participate fully in the workplace along with men, having to worry neither about comparable jobs nor about comparable value to the society in which they live.[21]

The radical feminist disagrees with both of the above approaches. She is unconvinced that either changes in the present law or changes in the political economy alone or in concert will solve the problem. She believes that changes must come from within the patriarchal family itself, the institution that fosters and reinforces the sexism that the radical feminist believes is at the heart of women's oppression. A change from capitalism to socialism, according to this view, does not change the nature of the sex stereotype that leaves women subordinate to men in the home and sexualized by them in almost every facet of life. While the radical feminist is sympathetic to the cry for consciousness-raising groups by the liberal feminist, she sees many of these as nothing more than middle-class therapy groups whose members go home feeling better, but who do nothing to promote lasting social change in such areas as childrearing and childcare, monogamous marriage, and compulsory heterosexuality. Such changes would not merely mean changes in the law or even changes in how people think, but changes within the structure of the family itself: (1) the end of the institution of motherhood where the woman is the primary if not sole caretaker of her children, in favor of either communal or shared parenting;[22] (2) the end of any taboo against other forms of marriage other than monogamous, heterosexual marriage; and (3) the end of the general taboo against homosexuality.[23] Lesbian separatists take the radical claim to require that women work, live, and make love primarily, if not solely, with other women as a means of tapping their creative spirit as women in the absence of the powerplay considered definitive of heterosexual relations.[24] In general, the radical feminist argues that men would no longer treat women as sex objects if their changes were implemented, because men would no longer be raised in or raise their children in a patriarchal and hierarchical setting in which women were classified as their right and proper subordinates in domestic, sexual, and economic life. With the burden of compulsory heterosexuality removed along with the sexual roles that such an orientation demands, men and women can be freed of their roles as sexual aggressors and passive receptors, mitigating the temptation for men to see themselves as the sexual subordinators of women.

The socialist feminist accepts many of the tenets of both Marxist and radical feminism in an attempt to synthesize the two into one coherent theory. She agrees with the Marxist feminist that major changes in our political economy are essential to ending the subordination of women to men, but also agrees with the radical feminist that such changes do not necessarily reach the patriarchal family structure in which the sexism that fosters women's oppression finds a safe haven. She advocates socialist reform and the restructuring of childcare, marriage, and the heterosexual family; women can then work in or out of the home with the assurance that they will not be treated as the subordinates of men. Thus, they can have the assurance that they will not be reduced (specifically) to sex objects.[25]

All these long-term proposals seek to make some fundamental changes in the ways men and women think about and act toward each other. Such changes, if successful, will be relatively more satisfying to those who object to sex objectification than the short-term alternatives listed above, because they attempt to reach the root causes of the problem. Yet because of this, each of them in its own way requires the kind of radical restructuring of contemporary norms that many persons, even those who may fall prey to sex objectification, are unwilling to make. Perhaps this is because many persons are more comfortable with the known, and many correctly see their own power and prestige in a capitalist economy dwindle with the changes that have been presented above. However, the arguments in this book have been that the sex objectification of women in contemporary culture is objectionable and that, therefore, social, economic, political, or psychological forces that seek to perpetuate it are themselves objectionable. Given the requirements concerning autonomy mentioned in Chapter II, any sexual ideology that succeeds in persuading persons to accept its dictates by means of intimidation, manipulation, social indoctrination, psychological domination, and the like is an ideology that violates the rights to live self-determined lives of those persons who are restricted by that ideology. Part of our present sexual ideology is the expectation that women will or ought to play the role of sex objects for men and that men will or ought to play the role of subordinators in sex. Because these role expectations involve intimidating, manipulating, or dominating many women — as well as men — into living the kinds of lives that they would not otherwise choose to lead, the lives of such persons are less autonomous than they might wish.

On the other hand, there are many persons who live in that same society who feel that such role expectations enhance their life choices or see nothing wrong or restrictive about the sexual expectations set for them. In Chapter II, it was suggested that while stereotypes may be unfavorable or restrictive, they certainly need not be. One might choose to live the very life one's ideology dictates even in the absence of it, and some women feel themselves lucky that, in the absence of other assets, they are valued primarily for their sexuality, even though they may lose their moral equality in the bargain. Men do not always regard an emphasis on performance as the ruination of a good sex life. We even saw from previous sections that there are many women who see their roles as sex objects as either lucrative or providing security or a good source of their self-esteem. Thus, the role expectations generated by the stereotypes implicit in our sexual ideology need not be oppressive to all persons. If these are the social realities, is there any one prevailing ideal in persons' sexual relations that would provide us with a model for social change? Since at least some people are unhappy with the sexual *status quo,* is there a kind of society or ideology that they might desire instead, that might be consistent with what those who enjoy the *status quo* desire?

5. MORAL EQUALITY AS A SEXUAL IDEAL

Suppose we were to adopt the ideal of moral equality in sexual relations. Such an ideal would dispense with sex objectification, since one must treat the person whom one treats as a sex object as less than a moral equal. Such an ideal would tend to facilitate trust and affection in sex, since neither partner acting on such an ideal would anticipate or promote the violation of the rights to well-being and freedom of the other. Such trust and affection in sex, as mentioned in Chapter II, would tend to foster intimacy in sex, which is a sexual ideal for many persons in contemporary society. However, even if one wished one's relations in sex to continue on a much less psychologically or emotionally involved level, the kind of trust that would be engendered by one's knowing one's rights to well-being and freedom would not be violated in those relations would carry the minimal presumption that one's partner would not inappropriately subordinate one's desires to her or his own.

I say *inappropriately* subordinate, because I think an ideal of moral equality can admit mutual consent to subordination or domination within the relationship *in a society which does not count such subordination, but rather counts moral equality as the status quo.* The problem we found with consent to such subordination was that, *given the prevailing sexual ideology,* it tended to foster and reinforce the view that women should be the subordinates of men, a view unduly restrictive of those who failed to agree with the ideology. But if the ideology were one of moral equality, no such subordination would be reinforced. In fact, since the rights to well-being and freedom of persons are based on what experiences they value in their lives, such an unequal relationship, if valued, and if not destructive of other non-subordinative relationships, could be justified on the same grounds as our rights to well-being and freedom. Thus, persons who found more sexual satisfaction in relations where one partner takes up a dominant or controlling role in the relationship would be free to do so. Such consent would be regarded as a consideration that justifies what would otherwise count as inappropriate treatment. So too, the self-stimulator could willingly subject herself to what would at present be considered her own sexual humiliation without the concern that such humiliation was considered proper for her or her choice of sex act. The point here is that the question of the morality of dominant/subordinate sexual relations is no longer a question of the appropriate action from within an already objectionable conceptual and moral framework, but of the appropriate action under a rubric of moral equality.

Such an ideal would also demand that we reject any Victorian mores about sex as demeaning to women, or any other sexual attitudes that place one person in a necessarily subordinate position to the other. A certain openness and honesty about sex would surely prevail in a society free of the associations of sex with sin or guilt (concomitant with such mores). It must remain an open question, however, as to whether one's sexual relations are to be essentially one's private affair or not, because privacy facilitates intimacy and spontaneity on the one hand, and also fosters a cloak of forbiddenness and illegitimacy about sex on the other.[26] But with an emphasis on understanding what one's partner desires out of the sex act, and with an emphasis on being honest about what emotional commitments or lack thereof one wishes to make in any of one's sexual relations, any privacy we maintain in sex may very well lose its more negative aspects. This will be especially true once we dispense with the notion that sex is necessarily demeaning or dirtying of any person.

However, without freedom from unjust subordination in the larger social spheres, we can hardly expect moral equality in the sexual sphere to hold out on its own. Whatever intimacy, honesty, or openness we pursue in our sexual relations, such pursuits must be accompanied by a kind of moral equality in the public sector in order to keep the sexual ideal itself from being subordinated to the political realities. Certainly, we cannot hope to change men's attitudes about women and about sex unless we also attack the larger institutions that foster and reinforce those attitudes. If such institutions do reinforce the sex objectification of women, and if they are guided by a general cultural ideology that (1) stereotypes women as the subordinates of men and (2) convinces men that if they give up subordinating women they will become subordinates themselves, it is no wonder that women have a difficult time persuading men not to treat them as sex objects.

Because the kind of social change demanded is so sweeping, any success at changing our stereotypes of men and women in sex is better than none at all. Such partial success is essential, because we can only change social institutions by (among other things) changing the attitudes of those persons who make up those institutions, and we can do that only by beginning with particular individuals, convincing them of our point of view, and then asking them to advocate their position to others. Such partial successes are tenuous at best; those women who entertain the attitude that they deserve to be treated as moral equals in their sexual relations must confront boyfriends, husbands, annd colleagues who think differently, and who may be used to having such women, as well as a host of their acquaintances, think differently. In addition, those men who find it objectionable to treat women as sex objects are often called effeminate, gay, or unmanly (meant as forms of degradation) by those whose stereotypes match the *status quo,* so any success at changing some attitudes can only heighten hostilities among those who disagree, often forcing those who reject the prevailing ideology to acquiesce in silence or be socially ostracized. Such changes appear necessary, and perhaps such hostilities inevitable, if we are to form a society in which moral equality in sexual relations is the rule and not the exception.

NOTES

1 Thomas E. Hill, Jr., "Servility and Self-Respect" in *Today's Moral Problems,* ed. Richard Wasserstrom (New York: Macmillan Publishing Company, 1975), p. 139.

2 *Ibid.,* p. 143.

3 For some of the ways in which a woman's socialization places options psychologically out of her reach, *see* Sharon Hill, "Self-Determination and Autonomy" in Wasserstrom, *op. cit.,* pp. 171–186.

4 *See* Richard B. Brandt, *Ethical Theory* (Englewood Cliffs, New Jersey: Prentice-Hall, 1959), pp. 410 and 446.

5 *See* W. K. Frankena, "Human Rights" in *Human Rights,* ed. A. I. Melden (Belmont, California: Wadsworth Publishing Company, 1970).

6 For a similar argument, see Mary Vetterling-Braggin's response to Betsy Postow in *Journal of the Philosophy of Sport* 8 (1981).

7 Compare what Judith Tormey says about the psychology of oppression in "Exploitation, Oppression, and Self-Sacrifice" in *Women and Philosophy,* ed. Carol C. Gould and Marx W. Wartofsky (New York: G. P. Putnam's Sons, 1976), p. 217.

8 Compare Sandra L. Bem and Daryl J. Bem, "Homogenizing the American Woman: The Power of an Unconscious Ideology" in *Feminist Frameworks,* ed. Alison M. Jaggar and Paula Rothenberg Struhl (New York: McGraw-Hill Book Company, 1978), p. 7: "We are very much like the fish who is unaware of the fact that his environment is wet. After all, what else could it be? . . . Such, in particular, is the nature of America's ideology about women."

9 The notion of "sex equality" is analyzed in some detail by Alison Jaggar, "On Sexual Equality" in *Sex Equality,* ed. Jane English (Englewood Cliffs, New Jersey: Prentice-Hall, 1977), pp. 94–109. *Also see* my list of feminist solutions to the problem of sex objectification, solutions that reveal the various ways in which feminists interpret the expression even within their own ranks.

10 *Newsweek* (October 24, 1983) under "Transitions."

11 For more on the ways in which the role of primary caretaker for husband and children contributes to a woman's anger, depression, and guilt, *see* Larry Blum, Marcia Homiak, Judy Housman, and Naomi Scheman, "Altruism and Women's Oppression," in *Philosophy and Women,* ed. Sharon Bishop and Marjorie Weinzweig (Belmont, California: Wadsworth Publishing Co., 1979), pp. 192ff.

12 For a detailed discussion of the way in which the present sexual division of labor functions to keep women subordinate to men, *see* Francine Rainone and Janice Moulton, "Sex Roles and the Sexual Division of Labor" in *"Femininity," "Masculinity," and "Androgyny,"* ed. Mary Vetterling-Braggin (Totowa, New Jersey: Littlefield, Adams, & Co., 1982), pp. 229ff.

13 For example, *see* James Rachels, "What People Deserve" in *Justice and Economic Distribution,* ed. John Arthur and William H. Shaw (Englewood Cliffs, New Jersey: Prentice-Hall, 1978), pp. 150–163.

14 Chief Justice Warren Burger has been known to refer to one of his associate Justices as "that O'Connor gal."

15 *See* Warren Farrell, *The Liberated Man* (New York: Random House, 1974), Chapter I. *Also see infra,* Chapter II, section 2C.

16 *See* Farrell, *op. cit.,* Chapter II.

17 *See* Janice Raymond, *The Transsexual Empire* (Boston: Beacon Press, 1979), esp. the preface, introduction, and Chapters II and V.

18 *See* Dorothy Dinnerstein, *The Mermaid and the Minotaur* (New York: Harper Colophon Books, Harper & Row, 1976), Chapter 10; *also see* Nancy Chodorow, *The Reproduc-*

tion of Mothering (Berkeley and Los Angeles, California: University of California Press, 1978), Afterword pp. 211-220.

19 However, there are those who disagree. Some might argue that the political institutions that foster sex objectification do so because the men who run those institutions are inherently the dominant members of the species; others might argue that to imagine matriarchy the way I have described it is simply to make women into men. *See* Lionel Tiger, *Men in Groups* (New York: Random House, 1969) who describes women as inherently incapable of the kind of "male-bonding" he considers necessary to public life. *Also see* Bruno Bettelheim, "Fathers Shouldn't Be Mothers," pp. 231-235 and Anthony Storr, "Aggression in the Relations Between the Sexes, pp. 278-279 in Jaggar and Struhl, *op. cit.*

20 *See* Maureen Reagan, "In Support of the ERA," and Patricia Cayo Sexton, "Workers (Female) Arise!" in Jaggar and Struhl, *op. cit.*, pp. 178-186.

21 *See* Margaret Benson, "The Political Economy of Women's Liberation" in Jaggar and Struhl, *op. cit.*, pp. 188-196; and *see* Juliet Mitchell, *Women's Estate* (New York: Random House, 1971).

22 *See* Dinnerstein and Chodorow, *op. cit.*

23 *See* Shulamith Firestone, *The Dialectic of Sex: The Case for Feminist Revolution* (New York: Bantam Books, 1970); *also see* Mary Daly, *Gyn/Ecology: the Metaethics of Radical Feminism* (Boston: Beacon Press, 1978). I have adopted the list of radical feminist concerns from Mary Anne Warren's summary of the position in her book *The Nature of Woman: An Encyclopedia and Guide to the Literature* (Inverness, California: Edgepress, 1980), p. 383.

24 *See* Radicalesbians, "The Woman Identified Woman," in *Radical Feminism,* ed. Anne Koedt, Ellen Levine, and Anita Rapone (New York: Quadrangle Books, 1973).

25 For arguments in favor of the socialist-feminist position, *see* Alison Jaggar, *Feminist Politics and Human Nature* (Totowa, New Jersey: Littlefield, Adams & Co., 1983).

26 For some competing considerations of the value of privacy in our society *see* Richard Wasserstrom, "Privacy: Some Arguments and Assumptions" in *Philosophical Law: Authority, Equality, Adjudication, Privacy,* ed. Richard Bronaugh (Westport, Connecticut: Greenwood Press, 1978), pp. 158ff.

chapter 5

Conclusions

In summary, then, what are the conclusions we have drawn from our analysis of the nature of, and objections to, sex objectification? First, we found that treating a person as a sex object is a form of dehumanization, viz. of treating a person as an object, but not also as a moral equal. One who is treated as less than a moral equal is either conceived of or acted toward as deserving less or none of the rights to well-being and freedom that persons capable of experiencing and valuing a certain level of well-being and freedom deserve. The man who treats a woman as a sex object, then, uses the sexuality of that person as the vehicle for denying her moral rights to well-being and freedom or giving otherwise *prima facie* insufficiently appropriate consideration to those rights. The women who treats herself as a sex object either conceives of herself as less than a moral equal or waives her rights to well-being and freedom in her sexual relations with others. Generally speaking, the sex objectifier of other persons is one who would willingly and *prima facie* inappropriately subordinate some or all of the desires of the person he or she finds sexually attractive to his or her own. The woman who is a self-objectifier, by waiving her rights, effectively permits some of or all of her own desires to be subordinated to someone else.

Because we place a premium in sex on some of the very rights or ideals that dehumanization denies—rights such as those to privacy or self-respect, or ideals such as intimacy and spontaneity— dehumanization in one's sexual relations seems especially objectionable. And because the dehumanization occurs in a sphere of personal relations that has significant sorts of social taboos and mores associated with it, any dehumanization in that sphere will at least come in contact with, if not directly violate, those taboos, and so be an especially significant form of dehumanization.

Furthermore, we found that the sex objectification of women in contemporary society typically forms a part of a broader, largely unconscious sexual ideology that stereotypes women as a class as the sexual subordinates of men, and that stereotypes men as the sexual dominators of women. In particular, because the prevailing stereotypes for women in sex were found unfairly to discriminate against women solely on the basis of their sex, the sex objectification of women that involved those stereotypes was considered sexist. We also found some reason for thinking that the sexual stereotypes for both women and men were not only unfavorable in content for many women and men, but also in danger of violating the rights of such persons to lead autonomous or self-determined lives. Such stereotypes were restrictive in this way when they fostered role expectations that intimidated, manipulated, indoctrinated, or psychologically dominated the persons who fell under the expectations to act in ways that they would not otherwise choose to act.

However, it was also suggested that persons could be held morally responsible for either treating other persons as sex objects or consenting to their own sex objectification, as long as they were free from the kinds of constraints suggested above. To the extent that any sexual ideology indoctrinates those who live under it to think and act in certain ways, such persons cannot be said to be fully responsible for their sex ojbectification. However, the claim was that persons who live under the prevailing sexual ideology, but who are not in some way coerced into conforming to it, are nevertheless in a position, as reflective, deliberative beings, to question its validity and to choose whether or not to follow its prescriptions. To the extent that persons in contemporary society can do this, they can and should be held morally responsible for choosing to treat persons as sex objects or consenting to be so treated.

It was also argued that the characterization of sex objectification presented in Chapters I and II is both more complete and more accurate than the characterizations that other philosophers have offered. In particular, the characterization suggests that men typically are not treated as *bona fide* sex objects by women, because sex is a much less effective vehicle for dehumanizing men than it is women. Also considered were various reasons why a woman might consent to her own sex objectification by others. The claim was that her free consent is typically not justified in a society where such consent only reinforces an already unfavorable and restrictive sexual stereotype of women (and of men). Voluntary and informed consent to one's own sexual subordination may be justified in isolation, or in a society in which the sexual ideology dictates moral equality, but it cannot be justified (or at least, not conclusively justified) given the prevailing social realities. In addition, there was some reason for thinking that the woman in contemporary society who permits her own sex objectification in some areas of her life but not others, may be tacitly encouraging sex objectification in just those areas in which she does not desire it. Given a sexual ideology that asserts that women are the proper sexual subordinates of men, those women who live under that ideology but who nevertheless do not think their preoccupation with appearing sexually attractive to men is part of a process of their dehumanization by men must shoulder the burden of proof.

We then suggested that an ideal of moral equality in sex, including a kind of candor and honesty in one's sexual relations, could be considered a kind of sexual ideal. However, to approach this ideal would mean a radical restructuring of our social, economic, and political institutions, since these institutions at present only reinforce moral inequality in the sexual sphere. Because men's and women's attitudes about their sexual relations with one another are so intimately tied to the structure of our larger political institutions, one begins to have some sympathy for the man or woman who would try to change the sexual attitudes of those who adhere to the prevailing ideology. Nevertheless, this is an important project to embark on, if we are to convince persons that it is *prima facie* inappropriate in contemporary society to treat oneself or other persons as sex objects.

Our sexual ideal involves the rights to well-being and freedom that are rights, not of an exclusively sexual sphere, but of morality as a whole. This fact became clear when, in Chapter I, we analyzed what it meant to dehumanize persons outside the sphere of sexual relations. However, a study of the ways in which sexual morality figures in our daily lives demands more than simply applying the rights to well-being and freedom of ordinary morality to one's sexual relations. We must also investigate the ways in which sex and specific sexual attitudes figure in the construction of the moral dilemma itself.

So, for example, some of our sexual attitudes involve beliefs in certain taboos and cultural mores that make sex a private, mysterious, frequently forbidden kind of affair. On the other hand, it is a sphere of our lives in which we can express affection and trust, and achieve a kind of sensual pleasure unmatched in other areas of our personal relations. Thus, we may feel it especially important to protect the pursuit of those endeavors in sex that are less important or not important at all in other personal relations of a more public or less intimate nature. As Sara Ruddick notes, "Often in our sexual lives, we neither flout nor simply apply general moral principles. Rather, the values of sexual experiences themselves figure in the construction of moral dilemmas." (*See* Sara Ruddick, "Better Sex" in *Philosophy and Sex,* ed. Robert Baker and Frederick Elliston [New York: Prometheus Books, 1975, p. 84.]) Thus, some attempt was made to capture why it is that sex objectification, as opposed to other forms of dehumanization, might carry with it the special or significant objections that it does. Furthermore, we have seen how our current sexual attitudes form part of a larger oppressive cultural framework with the potential for restricting the life-choices of those who would think or act other than the ideology dictates. The analysis of the nature of and objections to sex objectification therefore included an examination of the larger social context and prevailing sexual ideology in which the sex objectification occurs. Solely to apply the rules of morality proper to the issue of sex objectification would be to isolate the issue from its social context and from the prevailing sexual attitudes that define it. The morality of sex objectification, then, is but one of many issues in a study of sexual morality worthy of separate and detailed investigation.

Bibliography

Arthur, John, and Shaw, William H. *Justice and Economic Distribution*. Englewood Cliffs, New Jersey: Prentice-Hall, Inc., 1978.

Atkinson, Ronald. *Sexual Morality*. London: Hutchinson & Company, 1965.

Baker, Robert and Elliston, Frederick, ed. *Philosophy and Sex*. New York: Prometheus Books, 1975.

Barry, Kathleen. *Female Sexual Slavery*. Englewood Cliffs, New Jersey: Prentice-Hall, Inc., 1979.

Beardsley, Elizabeth L. "Determinism and Moral Perspectives." *Philosophy and Phenomenological Research* 21, No. 1 (September, 1960): 1–20.

Bishop, Sharon, and Weinzweig, Marjorie, ed. *Philosophy and Women*. Belmont, California: Wadsworth Publishing Company, 1979.

Brandt, Richard B., ed. *Social Justice*. Englewood Cliffs, New Jersey: Prentice-Hall, Inc., 1962.

Bronaugh, Richard, ed. *Philosophical Law: Authority, Equality, Adjudication, Privacy*. Westport, Connecticut: Greenwood Press, 1978.

Brownmiller, Susan. *Against Our Will: Men, Women, and Rape*. New York: Simon & Schuster, 1975.

Brunt, Rosalind, and Rowan, Caroline, ed. *Feminism, Culture and Politics*. London: Lawrence and Wishart, 1982.

Carlson, Neil R. *The Physiology of Behavior*. Boston: Allyn and Bacon, 1977.

Darwall, Steven L. "Two Kinds of Respect." *Ethics* 88, No. 1 (October, 1977): 36–49.

Dawkins, Richard. *The Selfish Gene*. Oxford: Oxford University Press, 1976.

Dinnerstein, Dorothy. *The Mermaid and the Minotaur*. New York: Harper & Row, 1976.

Downie, R. S., and Telfer, Elizabeth. *Respect for Persons*. London: Allen & Unwin, 1969.

Dworkin, Andrea. *Woman Hating*. New York: E. P. Dutton, 1974.

Dworkin, Ronald. *Taking Rights Seriously*. Cambridge, Massachusetts: Harvard University Press, 1977.

Eames, Elizabeth. "Sexism and Woman as Sex Object." *Journal of Thought* 11, No. 2 (April, 1976): 140–143.

English, Jane, ed. *Sex Equality*. Englewood Cliffs, New Jersey: Prentice-Hall, Inc., 1977.

Farrell, Warren. *The Liberated Man*. New York: Random House, 1974.

158   Bibliography

Fasteau, Marc Feigen. *The Male Machine*. New York: Dell Publishing Company, 1975.

Faust, Beatrice. *Women, Sex, and Pornography*. New York: Macmillan Publishing Company, 1980.

Firestone, Shulamith. *The Dialectic of Sex*. New York: Bantam Books, 1972.

Fisher, Peter. *The Gay Mystique*. New York: Stein & Day, 1972.

Flemming, Arthur. "Using a Man as a Means." *Ethics* 88, No. 4 (July, 1978): 283-298.

Fox, Michael. " 'Animal Liberation': A Critique." *Ethics* 88, No. 2 (January, 1978): 106-118.

Freud, Sigmund. *Civilization and its Discontents*. Translated and edited by James Strachey. New York: W. W. Norton & Company, 1961.

Fried, Charles. *An Anatomy of Values: Problems of Personal and Social Choice*. Cambridge, Massachusetts: Harvard University Press, 1970.

Friedan, Betty. *The Feminine Mystique*. New York: Dell Publishing Company, 1963.

Fritz, Leah. *Dreamers and Dealers: An Intimate Appraisal of the Women's Movement*. Boston: Beacon Press, 1979.

Frye, Marilyn. *The Politics of Reality: Essays in Feminist Theory*. Trumansburg, New York: The Crossing Press, 1983.

Goldberg, Steven. *The Inevitability of Patriarchy*. New York: William Morrow & Company, 1973.

Goldman, Alan. "Plain Sex." *Philosophy and Public Affairs* 6, No. 3 (Spring, 1977): 267-287.

Goodman, Bernice. *The Lesbian: A Celebration of Difference*. New York: Out and Out Books, 1977.

Gornick, Vivian, and Moran, Barbara K., ed. *Woman in Sexist Society*. New York: Basic Books, 1971.

Gould, Carol C., and Wartofsky, Marx W., ed. *Women and Philosophy*. New York: G. P. Putnam's Sons, 1976.

Haworth, Lawrence. "Rights, Wrongs, and Animals." *Ethics* 88, No. 2 (January, 1978): 95-105.

Hill, Thomas E., Jr. Book review of *Philosophy and Social Issues,* by Richard Wasserstrom. *UCLA Law Review* 28, No. 1 (October, 1980): 135-143.

_____. "Humanity as an End in Itself." *Ethics* 91, No. 1 (October, 1980): 84-99.

Jaggar, Alison M. *Feminist Politics and Human Nature*. Totowa, New Jersey: Littlefield, Adams & Company, 1983.

Jaggar, Alison M., and Struhl, Paula Rothenberg, ed. *Feminist Frameworks*. New York: McGraw-Hill Book Company, 1978.

Jenkins, Christie. *Buns: A Woman Looks at Men's*. New York: G. P. Putnam's Sons, 1980.

Kant, Immanuel. *Groundwork of the Metaphysics of Morals*. Translated by H. J. Paton. New York: Harper & Row, 1964.

_____. *The Metaphysical Principles of Virtue*. Translated by James Ellington. New York: Bobbs-Merrill Company, 1964.

Keodt, Anne, Levine, Ellen, and Rapone, Anita, ed. *Radical Feminism*. New York: Quadrangle Books, 1973.

Kolbenschlag, Madonna. *Kiss Sleeping Beauty Good-bye: Breaking the Spell of Feminine Myths and Models*. Garden City, New York: Doubleday & Company, 1979.

Korda, Michael. *Male Chauvinism! How it Works*. New York: Ballantine Books, 1973.

Lakoff, Robin. *Language and Woman's Place*. New York: Harper & Row, 1975.

Lyons, David, ed. *Rights*. Belmont, California: Wadsworth Publishing Company, 1979.

MacKinnon, Catharine A. "Feminism, Marxism, Method, and the State: An Agenda for Theory." *Signs: Journal of Women in Culture and Society 7,* No. 3 (Spring, 1982): 515-544.

MacKinnon, Catharine A. *Sexual Harassment of Working Women*. New Haven, Connecticut: Yale University Press, 1979.

Mahowald, Mary Brody, ed. *Philosophy of Women: Classical to Current Concepts*. Indianapolis: Hackett Publishing Company, 1978.

Marietta, Don E. "On Using People." *Ethics* 82, No. 3 (April, 1972):232–238.

Midgley, Mary. "The Concept of Beastliness: Philosophy, Ethics and Animal Behavior." *Philosophy* 48, No. 184 (April, 1973): 111–135.

Miller, Jean Baker, M.D., ed. *Psychoanalysis and Women*. New York: Penguin Books, 1973.

Miller, Jean Baker, M.D. *Toward a New Psychology of Women*. Boston: Beacon Press, 1976.

Millett, Kate. *Sexual Politics*. New York: Ballantine Books, 1969.

Money, John, and Ehrhardt, Anke A. *Man and Woman, Boy and Girl*. Baltimore: Johns Hopkins University Press, 1972.

Morgan, Robin, ed. *Sisterhood is Powerful*. New York: Vintage Books, 1970.

Nichols, Jack. *Men's Liberation: A New Definition of Masculinity*. New York: Penguin Books, 1975.

Postow, Betsy, C., ed. *Women, Philosophy and Sport*. Metuchen, New Jersey: The Scarecrow Press, 1983.

Raymond, Janice. *The Transsexual Empire: The Making of the She-Male*. Boston: Beacon Press, 1979.

Reiman, Jeffrey, H. "Privacy, Intimacy, and Personhood." *Philosophy and Public Affairs* 5, No. 1 (Fall, 1976): 26–44.

Reiter, Rayna R., ed. *Towards an Anthropology of Women*. New York: Monthly Review Press, 1975.

Richards, Janet Radcliffe. *The Sceptical Feminist*. Boston: Routledge & Kegan Paul, 1980.

Richards, Norvin. "Using People." *Mind* 87, No. 345 (January, 1978): 98–104.

Salper, Roberta, ed. *Female Liberation: History and Current Politics*. New York: Alfred A. Knopf, 1972.

Sartre, Jean-Paul. *Being and Nothingness*. Translated by Hazel E. Barnes. New York: Washington Square Press, 1966.

Sayers, Dorothy L. *Are Women Human?* Grand Rapids, Michigan: William B. Eerdmans Publishing Company, 1971.

Shaffer, Jerome. "Sexual Desire." *Journal of Philosophy* 75, No. 4 (April, 1978): 175–189.

Soble, Alan, ed. *Philosophy of Sex*. Totowa, New Jersey: Littlefield, Adams & Company, 1980.

Spelman, Elizabeth. "Treating Persons as Persons." *Ethics* 88, No. 2 (January 1978): 150–161.

Stoller, Robert J., M.D. *Sexual Excitement: Dynamics of Erotic Life*. New York: Pantheon Books, 1979.

Tannehill, Reay. *Sex in History*. New York: Stein & Day, 1980.

Tiger, Lionel. *Men in Groups*. New York: Random House, 1969.

Tolson, Andrew. *The Limits of Masculinity*. New York: Harper & Row, 1979.

Verene, D. P., ed. *Sexual Love and Western Morality*. New York: Harper & Row, 1972.

Vetterling-Braggin, Mary, ed. *"Femininity," "Masculinity," and "Androgyny."* Totowa, New Jersey: Littlefield, Adams & Company, 1982.

_____, ed. *Sexist Language*. Totowa, New Jersey: Littlefield, Adams & Company, 1981.

Vetterling-Braggin, Mary, Elliston, Frederick, and English, Jane, ed. *Feminism and Philosophy*. Totowa, New Jersey: Littlefield, Adams & Company, 1978.

Warren, Mary Anne. *The Nature of Woman: An Encyclopedia and Guide to the Literature*. Inverness, California: Edgepress, 1980.

Wasserstrom, Richard. *Philosophy and Social Issues.* Notre Dame, Indiana: University of Notre Dame Press, 1980.

———, ed. *Today's Moral Problems.* New York: Macmillan Publishing Company, 1975.

———, ed. *Today's Moral Problems,* 2d. ed. New York: Macmillan Publishing Company, 1979.

Williams, Bernard. *Problems of the Self: Philosophical Papers 1956–1972.* London: Cambridge University Press, 1973.

Wilson, Edward O. *On Human Nature.* Cambridge, Massachusetts: Harvard University Press, 1978.

Young, Robert. "Autonomy and Socialization." *Mind* 89, No. 356 (October, 1980): 565–576.

Index

Aquinas, Thomas, 75

Baker, Robert, 117–24
Bartky, Sandra Lee, 107–16, 123

Consciousness-raising, 51, 72–73, 144, 145
Consenting to being treated as a sex object. *See* Sex objectification, consenting to one's sex objectification by others.

de Beauvoir, Simone, 31–32, 115
Dehumanization: causal, 32–33; conceptual associations of harm with, 118, 119–23; conceptual associations of sex with, 120–23; in de Beauvoir, Simone, 32; definition of, 29–30; examples of, other than sex objectification, 30, 138–40; and exploitation of the sex object, 104–5; hypothetical, 33–34; in Kant, 20, 32, 37, 75; and masturbation, 75–76; and moral equality, 29–34, 35–36, 120–22, 135, 138–40, 152–54; versus (merely) using a person, 37, 104; versus objectification, 29, 33–34,

53, 118; and prostitution, 104–5; and rights to well-being and freedom, 30–31, 35, 53, 76–82, 95, 96, 127–29, 148, 152–53; in sex objectification, 29–30, 31, 35–36, 44, 53, 95, 117, 135, 152–53. *See also* Moral Equality; Objectification.

Eames, Elizabeth, 11, 103–7, 111, 123
Exploitation: definition of, 104; and dehumanization of the sex object, 103–6; and prostitution, 104–6; right against, 23

Feminism: encouraging public awareness of sex objectification, 73, 132; and sex equality, 73, 138; sex objectification and liberal, 144; sex objectification and Marxist, 144–45; sex objectification and radical, 144–45; sex objectification and socialist, 146
Freud, Sigmund, 75

Garry, Ann, 117–24

Kant, Immanuel, 20, 32, 37, 75